Autism and Asperger Syndrome

BUSTING THE MYTHS

D1551424

Autism and Asperger Syndrome

BUSTING THE MYTHS

Lynn Adams, PhD, CCC-SLP

PLURAL
PUBLISHING
— INC. —

SAN DIEGO
OXFORD
BRISBANE

PLURAL PUBLISHING
INC.

5521 Ruffin Road
San Diego, CA 92123

e-mail: info@pluralpublishing.com
Web site: http://www.pluralpublishing.com

49 Bath Street
Abingdon, Oxfordshire OX14 1EA
United Kingdom

Typeset in 11/13 Garamond by Flanagan's Publishing Services, Inc.
Printed in the United States of America by Bang Printing

Library of Congress Cataloging-in-Publication Data:

Adams, Lynn W.
  Autism and Asperger syndrome : busting the myths / Lynn Adams.
       p. ; cm.
  Includes bibliographical references and index.
  ISBN-13: 978-1-59756-083-2 (pbk.)
  ISBN-10: 1-59756-083-9 (pbk.)
  1. Autism—Patients—Rehabilitation. 2. Asperger's syndrome—Patients—
Rehabilitation. 3. Developmental disabilities.
  [DNLM: 1. Autistic Disorder—rehabilitation. 2. Asperger Syndrome—
rehabilitation. 3. Child. 4. Education, Special—methods. WM 203.5
A214a 2007] I. Title.
  RC553.A88A3376 2007
  616.85'882—dc22

                                                        2007010319

Contents

Preface

This book was inspired by the children with whom I have been fortunate enough to work over the last several years. The book is intended for both professionals and parents. I hope you find it informative and thoughtful.

If you are lucky enough to work with children with autism and Asperger syndrome, you are lucky enough. You are never bored, often challenged, and always thinking.

Acknowledgments

I acknowledge the children and families who have provided the experiences and challenges that made this book possible. Special thanks to those who allowed their children to serve as case studies. Thanks to the graduate students who helped with the preparation of the book, Karen Blankenship, Claire Conron, Tiaffany Gentry Katie Woods Newman, Bettheny Weeks O'Connell, and Karen Seigel, Christine Stewart, Diane Vinsh, and Alison Watters. Thanks to the Jesse Ball DuPont Foundation for its support of the Autism Center at Radford University. Thanks to my family who have supported me in all my endeavors, especially my move south.

This book is dedicated to Aileen and Chad Durham, along with their children Jackson and Sophie. Aileen and Chad—your constant support, love, and dedication to your son's well-being have served to inspire me for the past several years. I will carry you and your family in my heart forever. Thank you for allowing me to participate in your son's life.

Chapter 1

Autism and Asperger Syndrome

An Overview

Key Concepts

❖ Autism
  DSM-IVR
  Educational Description

❖ Asperger Syndrome
  DSM-IVR
  Educational Description

❖ Introduction ❖

What is it like to process the world differently than one's peers? How does the world look, sound, feel, and smell to a child with autism? Why do children with Asperger syndrome have such a hard time making friends? These questions are pondered by everyone who knows or works with children who have autism and Asperger syndrome. The more time you spend interacting with children with autism and Asperger syndrome, the closer you may get to the answers. That does not mean you will find the answers, but you may get closer.

Autism and Asperger syndrome were both initially described just over 50 years ago. Leo Kanner described autism in 1943 and Hans Asperger described the syndrome that bears his name in 1944. While professionals have been studying and treating autism since it was identified, Asperger syndrome is less understood and less examined. That is due, in part, to the fact that the Asperger article was not translated into English for many years. Asperger was from Eastern Europe and the prevailing political climate was not conducive to the sharing of scientific information until about 25 years ago (Wing, 1981). It was Wing who coined the term Asperger syndrome, and it was Wing who suggested that Asperger syndrome might be a variant of autism.

The bottom line is both are being diagnosed at an alarming rate that cannot be fully explained by the broader diagnostic criteria and better identification. There has been a huge increase in the number of children being served in the public schools under a label of autism. More research is needed. More professionals are needed. More training in the areas of identification, assessment, and communication intervention is needed. More public awareness is needed. More is needed!

❖ Characteristics of Autism ❖

What It Is and What It Isn't

Autism is defined as a lifelong developmental, neurobiological disorder marked by notable difficulty in communication and social relationships. It is a neurological disorder characterized by the presence of atypical behaviors including information processing differences, sensory processing problems, insistence on routine or sameness, and repetitive movements. Autism also includes problems with joint attention, social reciprocity, behavioral and emotional regulation, and language and cognitive deficits which include, but are not limited to, problems with communication, symbolic play, and executive functioning (ASHA, 2006; Tsai, 2000). Signs of autism are generally observable by 18 to 36 months of age (Neisworth & Wolfe, 2005). Once considered a rare disorder, autism went from an incidence rate of 1 in 1,000 (Bryson, 1997) to roughly 1 in 175 (CDC, n.d.). The diagnosis of autism is based on observable behaviors rather than a genetic evaluation or a medical test. Autism has been found everywhere across the world, in all socioeconomic levels, in all racial and ethnic groups.

All four developmental domains are impacted by autism, the sensory domain, the social domain, language, and cognition. The sensory domain includes the five traditional senses (hearing, smell, taste, vision, touch) as well as the vestibular sensory system. Children with autism may have disturbances in any or all six sensory systems, and to varying degrees (Grandin, 1992). Children with autism face social challenges daily as a result of their problems with language in communicative contexts, and the processing of social information.

Children with autism may have some degree of cognitive impairment, but traditional methods of assessing cognition rely on language processing and production, thereby impacting the accurate assessment of cognition. Autism is not a form mental retardation or a mental disorder, but it can be misdiagnosed as either and the resulting treatment is not likely to be effective (Fullerton, Stratton, Coyne, & Gray, 1996). Autism can co-occur with mental retardation (MR) and mental disturbance; however, the differential diagnosis of autism and MR can be complicated by the way MR is determined, specifically through the use of intelligence testing and measures of adaptive skills. Persons with autism do not always respond reliably, thereby complicating the assessment of cognitive and adaptive skills. Furthermore, the person with autism may not be able to effectively use the expressive language skills necessary to respond to traditional, language-based cognitive assessment. Additionally, the differential diagnosis of autism and schizophrenia can be complicated when the child is not able to report the presence of hallucinations.

Ultimately, autism is a disorder that changes over time. It is a dynamic problem that may manifest in certain behaviors at one age that disappear later. There is progress, and the occasional regression. The cause of regression is not known and the mechanism of regression is not fully understood. Some children regress when not enrolled in school or other intervention services. Others show regression of skills when they are ill. There are certainly ups and downs associated with the disorder itself and in the rearing of the child with autism. Children with autism can, with appropriate support and intervention, become adaptable people with a variety of skills and abilities. There is no one description that can adequately and correctly describe the course of this disorder in the life of the child.

What autism is not is a disorder of emotional disturbance in the typical sense. What that means is that, while people with autism have unusual emotional and behavioral responses to the world and its stimuli, they are not considered to be emotionally disturbed. However, we have seen a disturbing trend in recent years with some school systems in this area rejecting the diagnosis of autism or Asperger syndrome in favor of a label of emotional disturbance. This allows the school system to remove the child from the classroom for "problem behaviors" and place the child in both in-school and off-campus suspension programs.

Children with autism are not without emotions. It is patently false to consider them as lacking emotional responses. In fact, these children have a range of emotions including joy, fear, anger, and happiness; however, they tend to express these emotions in ways that are out of sync with what might be expected in a particular situation. It is this asynchrony that is often misinterpreted as a lack of emotion. On a related note, the child with autism may not respond to the social responses of others. The child may not respond to social praise or may ignore a reprimand. The child may be seemingly crushed by a simple correction (Your hair is messy), but remain unresponsive to a serious admonition (Do not run in the street).

Do children with autism actively avoid contact with other people? The simple answer is no. While they may interact with other people in a manner that seems like they are avoiding interaction, studies have shown that given the choice to be near another person versus a desired object, the children with autism chose to be near the other person (Frith, 1989). With regard to eye gaze, another myth associated with autism is that the child will actively avoid eye gaze. When presented with a human face, eyes open and eyes closed, and another picture of an object, the children with autism spent more time looking at the human face, regardless of whether the eyes were open or closed. Interestingly, they spent little time looking at anything for a sustained period. So why does the idea that eye gaze is avoided persist? According to Frith (1989) the reason is simple. The child will look fleetingly at a person and a file cabinet, but the file cabinet cannot complain! In other words, the child may not look at anything for a sustained period, but it is only another person who notices the limited eye gaze. What has been noted is that the child with autism does not make eye contact when expected and does not look away when expected. Ultimately, a lack of eye contact may have less to do with avoiding human contact and more to do with a lack of understanding of the conventions of conversation. Some adults with autism have reported that they found eye contact threatening. They shared that when others looked at them with direct eye contact, they felt challenged. They reported feeling stared at when eye contact lasted more than one or two seconds.

Another common misconception relative to autism is that persons with autism have special talents or skills, what is known as *savant syndrome*. Certainly savant syndrome can co-occur with autism and does so in about 5% of the population with autism (Randall & Parker, 1999), but the two are separate and distinct syndromes. Savant syndrome can result in dramatic musical abilities or calculation skills. Some savant skills include hearing a piece of music once and then playing it perfectly. Some with savant syndrome can complete complex mathematical calculations in their heads, often beating calculators to the answer. Calendar skills are also reported where the person with this type of savant skill can be given any date, either in the past or future, and can accurately name the day of the week upon which the date falls. We have not encountered people with both syndromes in our clinical practice over the past 20 years. We have encountered children and adults with some remarkable talents related to their narrow interests or foci.

Another myth with regard to autism is that all persons with autism engage in some form of self-injurious behavior. While many children with autism do scratch and bite themselves and bang their heads, not all with autism will present with self-harm. Along the same lines, it should be noted that some children engage in self-injurious behaviors in order to manipulate others. The child who bangs his head when not given a toy, but who is then given the toy after the head banging, may have learned that the head banging is an effective tool for getting desired results. Parents are often intimidated by the child's temper tantrums or "meltdowns," and the child can learn to use the threat of the meltdown as a way to manipulate the situation.

Autism is *not* the result of bad parenting or a lack of love and nurturing. It can be caused by anything that can impact the central nervous system (CNS) (Janzen, 2003). Conditions that have been implicated as causing the damage to the CNS include, but are not limited to, genetic factors, viral infections, hypoxia/anoxia during the birth or immediately following delivery, metabolic disorders, fetal drug and alcohol exposure, environmental toxins such as lead and mercury, and traumatic brain injury (TBI) (Gillberg, 1990; Gillberg & Coleman, 1992).

Rearing and living with the child with autism can produce significant stress for the parents and siblings. Studies have shown that autism creates more stress on the family than other disorders (Bagenholm & Gillberg, 1991; Fisman & Wolf, 1991). When compared to mothers of children with Down syndrome, mothers of children with autism reported poor attachment and less gratification from their children. This is likely directly due to the lack of responsiveness in the child with autism. Siblings of children with autism have reported feeling neglected with regard to positive parental attention. The siblings also reported having more responsibility for household chores and caregiving (Howlin, 1988). See Figure 1–1 for the medical description of autism.

Educational Description for Educational Diagnosis

For consideration of an educational label of autism, a child should demonstrate the following behavioral symptoms: (a) disturbances in the rate of appearance of physical, social, and language skills; (b) abnormal responses to sensations; (c) speech and language are absent or delayed, while specific thinking capabilities may be present; and (d) abnormal ways of relating to people, objects, and events.

A. A total of six (or more) items from (1), (2), and (3), with at least two from (1), and one each from (2) and (3):

   (1) qualitative impairment in social interaction, as manifested by at least two of the following:
       (a) marked impairment in the use of multiple nonverbal behaviors, such as eye-to-eye gaze, facial expression, body postures, and gestures to regulate social interaction
       (b) failure to develop peer relationships appropriate to developmental level
       (c) a lack of spontaneous seeking to share enjoyment, interests, or achievements with other people (e.g., by a lack of showing, bringing, or pointing out objects of interest)
       (d) lack of social or emotional reciprocity

   (2) qualitative impairments in communication, as manifested by at least one of the following:
       (a) delay in, or total lack of, the development of spoken language (not accompanied by an attempt to compensate through alternative modes of communication such as gesture or mime)
       (b) in individuals with adequate speech, marked impairment in the ability to initiate or sustain a conversation with others
       (c) stereotyped and repetitive use of language or idiosyncratic language
       (d) lack of varied, spontaneous make-believe play or social imitative play appropriate to developmental level

   (3) restricted, repetitive, and stereotyped patterns of behavior, interests, and activities as manifested by at least one of the following:
       (a) encompassing preoccupation with one or more stereotyped and restricted patterns of interest that is abnormal either in intensity or focus
       (b) apparently inflexible adherence to specific, nonfunctional routines or rituals

Figure 1–1. Description of autism. From *Diagnostic and Statistical Manual of Mental Disorders* (4th ed., text rev.) by American Psychiatric Association, 2000, Washington, DC: Author.

continues

    (c) stereotyped and repetitive motor mannerisms
        (e.g., hand or finger flapping or twisting or
        complex whole-body movements)
    (d) persistent preoccupation with parts of objects

  B. Delays or abnormal functioning in at least one of the
     following areas, with onset prior to age 3 years: (1) social
     interaction, (2) language as used in social
     communication, or (3) symbolic or imaginative play

  C. The disturbance is not better accounted for by Rett's
     disorder or childhood disintegrative disorder (APA, 2000).

Figure 1–1. *continued*

This description certainly addresses the same behaviors addressed in the *Diagnostic and Statistical Manual of Mental Disorders* (4th ed., APA, 2000) description, but this description emphasizes the communication and sensory deficits associated with autism.

While the Individuals with Disabilities Education Act (IDEA) has no specific guidelines mandating medical diagnoses of autism, some educational jurisdictions do not accept educational diagnoses. Rather, medical diagnoses are required in order for a child to be considered as having autism, and being eligible for intervention services. While states can interpret IDEA to meet their needs statewide, individual school systems can craft their own rules and regulations regarding the diagnosis of autism. For example, a school system in Virginia has determined that it will not accept a diagnosis of autism unless it was made by a developmental pediatrician or pediatric neurologist (J. Lingon, personal communication, June 15, 2006). The problem with this narrow interpretation is that it may disenfranchise those who do not have ready access to this type of medical professional. A review of medical professionals within a 100-mile radius of this system revealed one medical professional who met this system's requirements. His office reported a lag of 6 to 8 months from the time of referral to the assessment and diagnosis of one child (N. Rock, personal communication, October 23, 2006). The obvious solution is to have more personnel trained in the assessment and diagnosis of autism. Additionally, if nonmedical professionals can make diagnoses, the wait time for families may be reduced. Another route may be telemedicine. Using technology to link a family who is far from services to the professional who can assess and diagnose may facilitate the process.

❖ Characteristics of Asperger Syndrome ❖

What It Is and What It Isn't

Asperger syndrome may be a variant of autism or it may be a separate but related disorder. That is of less importance to understand than to recognize that while autism and Asperger syndrome have a great deal in common, they also have a number of differences that must be understood and addressed.

By around 6 years of age, children with Asperger syndrome do not differ significantly from those with high functioning autism. Macintosh and Dissanayake (2004) determined that there is not sufficient evidence to support the notion of Asperger syndrome as a distinct disorder relative to high functioning autism. The cognitive profiles of children with Asperger syndrome have demonstrated higher verbal IQs relative to performance IQs (Volkmar, Lord, Bailey, Schultz, & Klin, 2004). Two other studies using the DSM-IV criteria for the differential diagnosis of Asperger syndrome and high functioning autism noted that, as a group, persons with Asperger syndrome had higher verbal IQs than the individuals with high functioning autism; however, there was sufficient variability at the individual level to note that higher verbal IQs were not unique to those with Asperger syndrome (Ghaziuddin & Mountain-Kimchi, 2004; Miller & Orzonoff, 2000).

Of particular interest is the differentiation of Asperger syndrome from bipolar disorder or any comorbid issue. Recently it was noted that children with Asperger syndrome were being misdiagnosed as having bipolar disorder and, as a result, were being treated with medications that might not be effective. Misdiagnosing the disorder prevents children from receiving proper treatment and learning important skills for success in social settings, school, and relationships. While a diagnosis can be made for Asperger syndrome as early as 2 years old, most children are not diagnosed until they reach middle school or later. "There is a huge confusion over what Asperger is and what it isn't because it has only been diagnosed by the present criteria for the past 12 years," says Dan Hoover, PhD, a psychologist with the Adolescent Treatment Program at the Menninger Clinic and associate professor in the Menninger Department of Psychiatry & Behavioral Sciences at Baylor College of Medicine. "Asperger is over diagnosed by some clinicians who are looking for it, and missed by clinicians who don't know what to look for, or who do not want to give their patients the label of having Asperger syndrome" (Schafer Autism Report, 2006). One point of differentiation that we have found, and are in the process of examining, is the response to verbal-based humor. We have noted through observation and a pilot project that young adults with Asperger syndrome differ from those with bipolar disorder in their response to word play found on greeting cards. When presented with cards that demonstrate word play or puns, the subjects with Asperger syndrome did not understand why the card was supposed to be funny and required explicit feedback to comprehend the jokes, while those with bipolar disorder readily understood the humor in the cards.

There is evidence to support a comorbid relationship between Asperger syndrome and a number of other disorders. These include obsessive-compulsive disorder, depression, Tourette's syndrome, affective disorders, attention problems, and psychosis (Volkmar & Klin, 2000). So, while Asperger syndrome can co-occur with psychiatric disorders, the differential diagnosis should be carefully completed to ensure accurate and effective treatment planning, which may include medication and behavioral/talk therapy.

Children referred to our center often come with a long list of "related" problems. This list can include attention deficit disorder (with and without hyperactivity), central auditory processing disorders, oppositional-defiant disorder, obsessive-compulsive disorder, and a variety of other anxiety disorders. While it is reasonable with Asperger syndrome can co-occur with any and all of these other disorders, it is important to note that the characteristics of Asperger syndrome include behaviors commonly associated with all the preceding "related" problems. What is of concern is that the "laundry list" is often daunting, confusing, and overwhelming to the parents of the child with Asperger syndrome.

Asperger syndrome creates learning challenges for the child. Inattentiveness and distractibility impact the child in the classroom.

Children with Asperger syndrome tend to have difficulty in determining figure ground in that they often have trouble determining what is important in a situation or scene, focusing on minute details but missing the point. Children with Asperger syndrome often demonstrate extremely narrow focus or attention or tunnel vision (Myles & Simpson, 2003). Because there can be so much stimulation in the classroom, the child with Asperger syndrome may focus on one aspect of the class to the exclusion of all other stimuli. The child with Asperger syndrome may focus on the text because it is of high interest and ignore the class discussion of the text. While the child may memorize the text, he will not have integrated the discussion into his understanding, thereby limited his knowledge of the topic.

Persons with Asperger syndrome are often visual learners rather than auditory learners. Because of this, the child may not appear to struggle in school until the curriculum becomes more lecture or discussion based. He or she may manage the classroom curriculum well when visual support is available, but become lost when that level of contextualization is missing. Along the same lines, the child with Asperger syndrome may be able to handle the demands of the classroom while there is sufficient structure. With the increase in grade level, usually around fourth or fifth grade, comes a decrease in structure. This is meant to coincide with social maturation that occurs at this age level. Unfortunately for the child with a need for structure, routine, and rules, this can be an exceptionally challenging time. Children with Asperger syndrome who never had "behavior" problems may suddenly become irritable and frustrated and begin acting out.

Children with Asperger syndrome are often described as rude, belligerent, and disrespectful in the school setting. These problems may result from what is referred to as the "hidden curriculum" (Myles & Simpson, 2003). The hidden curriculum refers to the slang of the students, and the rules that "everyone knows" but that are not explicitly stated. Some teachers allow quiet discussion in the room while another does not, but neither teacher has those rules posted. The child with Asperger syndrome is not likely to understand what behaviors are pleasing to the teacher, as the child with Asperger syndrome is egocentric in his thinking, and does not know the teacher needs to be pleased. The hidden curriculum of the community includes things like not talking to strangers, but a policeman is a stranger and if he is asking the child with Asperger syndrome a question, he is expecting an answer. Children with Asperger syndrome usually have all or nothing rules, very black and white distinctions that do not allow for exceptions (Myles & Simpson, 2001). Figure 1-2 includes the complete diagnostic criteria for Asperger syndrome.

Educational Description for Educational Diagnosis

Currently, no educational description for Asperger syndrome exists. This is a crucial omission as the educational implications associated with Asperger syndrome are numerous and can be extremely complex. While children demonstrating autism may be readily diagnosed by age 3 years, children with Asperger syndrome are often not recognized as having a problem until age 6 or 7 years or later. Perhaps the educational description for Asperger syndrome could follow that of Wing (1998) where eight characteristics of Asperger syndrome were delineated:

1. Socially odd, naïve, and inappropriately emotionally detached from others

2. Markedly egocentric and highly sensitive to others' criticism, but apparently oblivious to others' feelings

3. Excellent grammar and vocabulary with fluent speech, but often literal and pedantic, engaging in monologues versus dialogues (conversations)

4. Notably poor nonverbal communication and unusual prosody

5. Intense interest in specific subjects

6. Borderline to gifted IQ and excellent skills relative to specific areas of interest, but difficulty with conventional schoolwork

7. Awkward and clumsy

8. Lacking in common sense

This list addresses the areas of concern with regard to Asperger syndrome that are likely to impact successful performance in the classroom, and the list may serve as a meaningful description for educational service planning. Educational service planning is often

A. Qualitative impairment in social interaction, as manifested by at least two of the following:

   (1) marked impairment in the use of multiple nonverbal behaviors, such as eye-to-eye gaze, facial expression, body postures, and gestures to regulate social interaction

   (2) failure to develop peer relationships appropriate to developmental level

   (3) a lack of spontaneous seeking to share enjoyment, interests, or achievements with other people (e.g., by a lack of showing, bringing, or pointing out objects of interest to other people)

   (4) lack of social or emotional reciprocity

B. Restricted, repetitive, and stereotyped patterns of behavior, interests, and activities, as manifested by at least one of the following:

   (1) encompassing preoccupation with one or more stereotyped and restricted patterns of interest that is abnormal either in intensity or focus

   (2) apparently inflexible adherence to specific, nonfunctional routines or rituals

   (3) stereotyped and repetitive motor mannerisms (e.g., hand or finger flapping or twisting, or complex whole-body movements)

   (4) persistent preoccupation with parts of objects

C. The disturbance causes clinically significant impairment in social, occupational, or other important areas of functioning.

D. There is no clinically significant general delay in language (e.g., single words used by age 2 years, communicative phrases used by age 3 years).

E. There is no clinically significant delay in cognitive development or in the development of age-appropriate self-help skills, adaptive behavior (other than in social interaction), and curiosity about the environment in childhood.

F. Criteria are not met for another specific pervasive developmental disorder or schizophrenia.

Figure 1–2. Description of Asperger syndrome. From *Diagnostic and Statistical Manual of Mental Disorders* (4th ed., text rev.), by American Psychiatric Association, 2000, Washington, DC: Author.

challenging for the child with Asperger syndrome. This child may not readily qualify for special educational services given that many with Asperger syndrome have IQs which fall in the above average to gifted range with academic achievement in the low average to average range. Conventional thinking may be that if one is intellectually gifted and presenting with average academic achievement, no intervention is warranted. This shortsightedness can lead to a lack of services for the child with Asperger syndrome. Social skill deficits may not be addressed in the educational setting, but it is imperative that this aspect of Asperger syndrome be addressed as social deficits can certainly impact educational performance. The child with Asperger syndrome may not participate in the classroom setting in a manner that is reflective of his or her ability level. For example, Jason was readily able to participate in most class discussions, but he did not seem to recognize the need to do so. Since his grade in class was based in part on his participation in discussions, his lack of participation pulled his grade down. He needed direct instruction to raise his hand and actively participate in class discussions.

❖ Discussion Starters ❖

1. How are autism and Asperger syndrome similar? How do they differ?

2. What challenges might a family with a child with autism or Asperger syndrome face?

3. What would you see as your role in serving the child and family that are impacted by autism or Asperger syndrome?

Chapter 2

Autism: A Look at the Puzzle

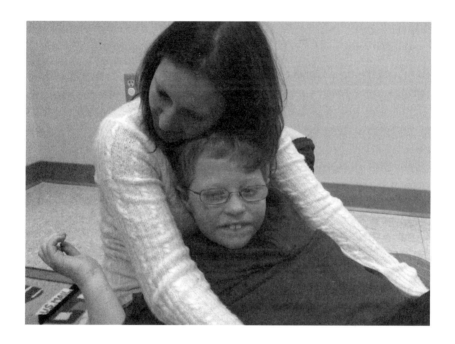

Key Concepts

❖ Cognitive Abilities
   Information Processing
   Memory
   Theory of Mind

❖ Linguistic Abilities
   Comprehension
   Production

Prosody
Idioms

❖ Social Abilities

❖ Sensory and Motor Skills

❖ Academic Skills

❖ Autism ❖

Persons with autism present with a variety of challenges in terms of cognitive functioning, learning, language use, social interaction, and sensory motor functioning. There is no one-size-fits-all description to be provided, so one must approach the following information as general descriptions of autism. It will ring true for most but not all.

❖ Cognitive Abilities ❖

Can IQ scores obtained for children with autism be trusted? Are they valid? Do they measure *test* intelligence or *world* intelligence? Children with autism are difficult to test in light of attention, processing, and motivational concerns. There is general consensus that children with autism present a more jagged profile on the subtests of published intelligence measures. Usually, performance is most compromised on those subtests that require a high degree of communicative competence, and the highest level of performance is noted on subtests requiring figure recreation (Frith, 1989). Caution is always prescribed when interpreting data obtained through standardized testing.

Researchers have found that persons with autism have a different cognitive style. This difference is the result of incomplete information processing. Information is taken in but little analysis or integration occurs (Fullerton, Stratton, Coyne, & Gray, 1996). Using this approach, the entire event may be stored in detail without the meaning of the event being extracted. Janzen (2003) used an analogy of a video camera to illustrate the processing of the brain of the person with autism. The camera just records all that occurs in front of it. It cannot edit out the extraneous and every item is recorded with the same focus. It is up to the user to determine the figure and the ground, the important and the superfluous. The person with autism cannot "edit" the tape to delete the unimportant, but rather, the person simply stores all the information randomly and without integration. This interpretation leads to the discussion of the information processing model for cognition.

The information processing model of cognition requires one to attend, discriminate, organize, remember/recall, and generalize incoming information. For the child with autism, the difficulty in processing information begins with the first step, attending. It may not be that the child cannot attend, but attends to the wrong things, peculiar things (Frith, 1989). Given that, one will expect the child with autism to have difficulty with most, if not all, incoming information. Should the child be able to attend sufficiently, discrimination (ignoring extraneous stimuli while attending to pertinent stimuli) will likely prove problematic. Children with autism may focus too much attention on all the details, essentially losing the forest for the trees. Organization will probably not be difficult if the child can attend and discriminate. A relative strength for the child with autism is in memory and recall; however, getting to this point in the process is most challenging. Finally, generalization is not likely if the information has not been fully processed (Klinger & Dawson, 1992). Courchesne et al. (1994) noted that children with autism have difficulty controlling and directing attention to some information while attending quite intensely to one limited aspect of information. This tendency results in information that "lacks context and temporal continuity" (p. 20).

As a result of the child's difficulty with attention, discrimination, and organization, learning is compromised in that erroneous associations can be made. The child may form a false association, believing that unrelated events are in fact related. For example, if the door bell rings at the same time the computer Internet system fails, the child may assume a cause and effect relationship that was merely the result of coincidence. It has been suggested that the nonfunctional routines and ritualistic behaviors associated with autism are the result of this type of learning (Janzen, 2003).

Information which is learned and stored via the compromised information processing system may not be stored and accessed in an appropriate sequence. This can result in problems with relating events and incidents. It can impair the child's ability to learn from behavioral consequences and can severely impair the formation or accurate cause and effect relationships as well as the development of essential means to end concepts.

Finally, problem solving, highly dependent on generalization or transfer of learning, is impaired in the child with autism. If one has not been successful in attending and organizing information, the ability to make judgments and reason will be impacted. One school of thought is that the child with autism does not recognize the need for generalization and therefore does not generalize learning to new and novel events. This is especially evident in the problem solving skills of children with high functioning autism. Children with high functioning autism demonstrate intellectual potential that would lead one to expect effective reasoning and judgments, but they are often unsuccessful in this regard. Children with autism have particular learning strengths that can facilitate their successful performance in school and other settings. These strengths include excellent memory and recall, visual learning, preference for the routine and rote, conformation to rules, and attention to areas of interest (Janzen, 2003).

An aspect of cognition receiving great attention recently is *theory of mind.* Theory of mind involves the ability to think about other people's thinking. According to theory of mind, an individual's understanding of him- or herself and others contributes to, and is restricted by, the knowledge and beliefs about the mental world (Adams, 2005). Baron-Cohen (1990) explains the use of epistemic and mental state words in a common example.

> A man comes out of a shop and walks off down the street. About half-way down the street he suddenly stops, turns around, runs back to the shop, and goes inside. (We must understand that the man must have remembered he has left something in the shop, that he wants to retrieve it, and that he believes it will still be in the shop). The man then re-emerges from the shop, but this time he walks along slowly, scanning the ground. (Now we make the assumption that whatever he thought was in the shop was not there, and that he now believes he may have dropped it on the pavement outside) (Baron-Cohen, 1990, p. 86).

This example clearly illustrates the thought process the man went through, in addition to what an onlooker's perspective of the situation may be. The man's actions would seem unusual if we lacked the ability to understand mental state terms.

With an underdeveloped theory of mind, an individual may interpret a message literally and intended cues, such as sarcasm, are not perceived as the speaker intended. It is the listener's responsibility to interpret the verbal and nonverbal intentions of the speaker. It is the speaker's responsibility to monitor whether the intended meaning is received correctly or if a repair in the conversation is needed. When there are gaps in communication, the ability to mind read is an important aspect of effective communication and helps an individual understand social situations and to predict behavior (Watters, 2005).

❖ Linguistic Abilities ❖

Language, made up of phonology, semantics, syntax, morphology, and pragmatics, in the child with autism has been assessed and studied with one universal finding, pragmatic deficits are a universal feature of autism. Children with autism vary in their abilities to acquire the segmental aspects of language, sounds, word meanings, and word order rules, but all will demonstrate some degree of impairment in the use of language as a social communication tool.

Children with autism may not acquire language skills like their peers. They may have difficulty with vocabulary acquisition. Children with autism may not realize that words carry meaning and function and, as a result, they do not use words to obtain attention or objects. Some children with autism develop a highly specific, idiosyncratic vocabulary which does not include multiple meanings for words or multiple labels for items. Some words are impacted by the context in which they are used. For example, the meanings of the words *here* and *there* change depending on the speaker's proximity to the item; however, the proximity of the listener does not impact the meanings. These context-specific words can be troubling to the person with autism.

Prosody, or the intonations and rhythms used to enhance meaning while speaking, can be problematic for the child with autism. The ability to understand prosody as well as to use prosody effectively has been shown to be deficient in this population. Some children with autism are described as speaking in a monotonic fashion while others have been noted to use a "game show host" prosodic pattern. Whether monotonic or exaggerated, it appears that the child with autism is not using prosody to enhance the semantic content of the spoken message. With regard to comprehension, children with autism have been found to have significant difficulty recognizing sarcasm and humor. Being literal, these children will take the speaker's words at face value and will not understand that the speaker might be joking or teasing.

Gesture development, a prerequisite for oral language use, has been found to be deficient in children with autism. They use fewer total gestures and fewer different gestures. One gesture that is used by most children with autism is "using another person as a tool." This has been noted with great frequency among young children with autism. Parents report that their child will take their hand and place it on the desired object or to note a desired outcome. For example, the child may place the parent's hand on the refrigerator to note the desire for a drink. He or she may place the hand on the doorknob to indicate a desire to go outside. Parents report feeling that the child is treating them like a disembodied hand, not a whole person. Why does the child do this? Maybe the child recognizes that the hand is what makes things happen. Maybe the child realizes that the hand is a much more powerful tool than the mouth, which may just serve as a food receptacle.

Idiomatic language is also difficult for the child with autism to comprehend and use effectively. Hearing "It is raining cats and dogs" might cause the child with autism to run to the window to view the spectacle only to be disheartened when water is the only thing falling from the clouds. The comment, "He ran his heart out," may cause the child with autism to respond with "Yuck." Jerry, a 9-year-old boy, described his friend, Joe, who just wanted to watch TV instead of play outside, as "a potato on the couch."

Because cognition and language are inextricably linked, deficits in one can impact the other. This is particularly true with regard to time concepts. Children with autism have great difficulty with the abstraction of time and this can impact their language skills, resulting in perseverative questioning or other repetitive language production. Children with autism comprehend and produce literal language. A verbose child with high functioning autism was told by a teacher that the teacher "did not like his mouth." The child took great offense at this as he knew he could do nothing to change the physical appearance of his mouth. He became a behavior problem in the classroom until the matter was resolved.

Theory of mind impacts communication. Effective communication is achieved when the speaker and listener utilize a theory of mind to structure the conversation. This includes using pragmatic knowledge to organize the information to be communicated in the most useful manner. The speaker must remember what the listener knows about a topic in order to include appropriate and nonredundant information. In addition, the speaker must know how to organize a series of utterances to make the discourse as comprehensible as possible (Baron-Cohen, O'Riordan, Stone, Jones, & Palisted, 1999). Without this perspective taking, the speaker may not be able to communicate effectively. It is important to understand that children who demonstrate social-communication deficits can be significantly impaired relative to their ability to function in the primary social setting.

When theory of mind is acquired and the individual is able to interpret the behaviors and intentions of others, the language he or she uses will be rich in epistemic or mental state words. Epistemic words are words that reflect inner conditions or internal actions in which an individual has acquired some knowledge. These terms fall into several categories, including nouns (e.g., idea, knowledge), verbs (e.g., think, believe, feel, want, hope, remember), adjectives (e.g., happy, thoughtful), and adverbs (e.g., sadly, wishfully) (Baron-Cohen et al., 1999). These epistemic words help an individual interpret his or her thought processes and the thought processes of others (Blankenship, 2000). Epistemic words are necessary to understand what other individuals think in a particular situation (Watters, 2005).

Without a theory of mind, society may seem disorganized and confusing (Baron-Cohen, 1999). Blankenship (2000) illustrated that epistemic words are frequently used in children's stories such as "Snow White" and "Little Red Riding Hood." If a child does not have an understanding of epistemic terms, he or she would not be able to understand the plot of the story and cannot take the perspective of the characters. Epistemic words are integral to the successful function in daily life.

Echolalia is a commonly observed behavior among children with autism. Because the child's information processing may be compromised, language processing can be negatively impacted as well. The child may be asked a question, but because of the processing difficulty, may only echo the question back to the asker. Because of incomplete processing, the child may echo previously heard utterances which are used with communicative intent (Prizant,

1983). Echolalia generally falls into three categories, immediate, delayed, and mitigated. Immediate echolalia occurs when the child repeats what someone says immediately after the speaker. Delayed echolalia occurs when the child repeats something heard earlier in a new context. Mitigated echolalia can be either immediate or delayed, but the child changes the original utterance slightly. It is important to note that echolalia is a useful behavior in that it can be shaped into functional communication. Mark, a 10-year-old boy with moderate autism, was echolalic. He enjoyed bubbles and would echo the clinician when she modeled "bubbles." Gradually, the modeled utterance was lengthened ("want bubbles," "want more bubbles") until he said "I want more bubbles" every time he wanted more. The cue was extinguished and he used delayed echolalia to request the activity.

A combination of echolalia and theory of mind can explain pronoun reversals often noted in the language production of children with autism. One reason a child may reverse pronouns results from delayed echolalia. The child may say "You want to go outside" instead of "I want to go outside" simply because that is what was said to the child the day before when he wanted to go outside. The more complex explanation results from theory of mind difficulties. An aspect of pronoun usage is what is known as the deictic function of pronouns. The use of specific pronouns relates to who is speaking and who is listening. This is known as shifting reference. Sometimes I am the speaker and sometimes I am the listener and pronouns change relative to my role in the conversation. The words *here* and *there* are also affected by deixis or shifting reference and can confound the child with autism. When I am near the desk, the desk is *here*, but as I move away from the desk, the desk is *there*. Similarly, the use of tense markers may be impaired in the child with autism. In order to use tense markers effectively, the speaker must constantly monitor and rapidly adjust the tense of verbs.

A review of the literature addressing speech sound production problems in children with autism indicates that some children who produce limited oral output may be experiencing significant articulation difficulties. Adams (1998) and Adams and Vinsh (2003) examined the motor speech skills in children with high functioning autism and autism. They found that some children in both groups had difficulty producing multisyllabic structures, consonant clusters, and presented with groping of the articulators.

❖ Social Abilities ❖

Social deficits in autism have been thoroughly described. The range of these deficits is wide and the manifestation of these deficits is varied. Some children with autism rarely, if ever, speak to another person. Others will speak to total strangers about topics that may be unrelated to the situation. In early childhood, the child with autism may be described as "in her own world" or she may tend to "look right through people." As the child gets older, it is often noted that he may lack modesty or shame. Behaviors that are considered taboo in "polite" society may be lost on the child with autism. Parents of children with autism can relate to the challenge of trying to teach their child not to pick his nose, not to scratch some body parts, and not to expel noxious odors!

It has been noted that persons with autism are not very adept at lying to or deceiving others. They tend not to engage in gossip. Rather than gossiping, the person with autism is more likely to tell a person she has bad breath directly versus telling someone else. The person with autism is often described as brutally honest, and without guile. Some with autism may be upset by the suffering of another. Casey, a 9-year-old female, became distraught when a nonautistic peer playfully teased a younger child at a day camp. Casey scolded the teaser, and positioned herself between the two children to protect the younger child. If the teaser, who was much larger than Casey, had taken offense, Casey could have been seriously harmed.

It is important to note that the social deficits in the child with autism are likely a direct result of their concomitant cognitive, sensory, and language deficits. In order to be effective in the social realm, one must understand both concrete and abstract concepts, be able to problem solve, be able to take another's perspective, read body language, process information, and ignore extraneous noises and sights. That monumental task is achieved by most people without any direct instruction, while the child with autism will require direct instruction and multiple repetitions in order to begin to demonstrate socially appropriate skills.

Direct instruction means just that, explicit teaching of the skills needed for appropriate social functioning. The child will require clear and functional teaching of social skills in the environment where the skills are to be used. For example, if the child needs to learn to negotiate the playground, the skills needed must be practiced on the playground. One cannot expect to teach skills in another setting (classroom, therapy room), and have those skills generalize to the actual target setting. Certainly, skills can be practiced in a therapy room and then practiced in the actual setting, but efficacy would dictate that these skills be addressed where they are needed.

There are a variety of strategies available to address the social needs of children with autism. Not all have a sufficient evidence base to endorse their use. Several strategies with emerging empirical support will be discussed in Chapter 5.

❖ Sensory and Motor Skills ❖

A significant amount of the professional literature has been dedicated to the sensory difficulties and deficits noted in children with autism. Delacato (1974) offered that premise that children with autism are hyper- or hyposensitive, and these sensory levels can vary within the child from hour to hour, and day to day. He discussed the child who could be hypersensitive in terms of hearing and might respond badly to loud sounds. The same child might appear hyposensitive to sound and not respond to her name. Children with autism have been described as being tactilely defensive, rejecting touch and often clothing. Temple Grandin (1986) described the calming effect of deep pressure she found when she climbed in a squeeze shoot used with cattle, located on her aunt's ranch. She went as far as to build a prototype for her personal use while in school. This type of "squeeze machine" is now available for use with persons with autism. A machine is not necessary, however, as some with autism respond well to bear hugs and being swaddled in a blanket. Hugs and swaddling do require another person to be implemented, while the squeeze machine allows the person with autism to direct the amount and duration of the pressure and when it is applied.

Conventional thinking has been that motor skills are not significantly impaired in children with autism. While gross and fine motor skills may not be impaired in terms of strength and range of motion, the initiation and cessation of movements may be impaired. Additionally, the fluidity of such movements may be problematic. Donna

Williams, a woman with high functioning autism, described being unable to go to the restroom unless someone else moved to the restroom first. She further described not being able to manage her own body language, finding herself imitating the body movements of her conversational partner, rather than using her own movements (Williams, 1992, 1994). Executive function (planning, organizing, and executing events) problems may contribute to these motor difficulties.

Some children with autism are described as being motorically advanced relative to the other skills domains. In this regard, the child may walk before talking. The child may run, dart, and lunge, often causing great fear and worry for the parent as the child may run and dart near traffic. A young child named Zach was referred for assessment at age 18 months. A home visit was completed. Zach was observed to be, literally, climbing the walls. Because of the coarse paneling and his ability, Zach was able to scale the walls of the living room, climbing several feet off the ground. As a consequence of his propensity for climbing, there were no window coverings in the house as he had tried, unsuccessfully, to climb the drapes and blinds first and all had been pulled down by him. His mother expressed concerns about his physical safety.

❖ Academic Skills ❖

Given the range of impairment that can accompany autism, the academic skills of persons with autism cannot be characterized with general descriptions. Rather, each person must be assessed and observed in order to determine academic strengths and needs. Those who work with persons with autism recognize that they will likely excel in academic areas that mirror their narrow interests. For example, the child who is focused on weather may excel in science, but only when meteorology is being discussed. Some children with autism demonstrate precocious letter and number identification skills, but lack the understanding of the underlying concepts.

Learning strengths associated with autism include memory, gestalt processing (processing the whole), visual processing, understanding the concrete, rule and routine orientation, and narrow interests. Learning challenges can include organization and executive function, auditory processing, analysis and synthesis, comprehension of abstract concepts, strict adherence to rules, heightened anxiety, language processing and production, and effective communication (Janzen, 2003).

Teachers can facilitate success in the classroom by considering a number of strategies. These include using visual supports including schedules and picture-communication systems, providing a defined work area, including sensory breaks for the child who needs them, recognizing rising frustration and defusing it, making sure all staff are fully informed and trained, and being flexible. An expanded discussion of academic skill development, assessment, and facilitation follows in Chapter 3.

❖ Case Studies ❖

Jake came to our clinic as a 23-month-old who was not talking. A review of his history revealed that he had developed a vocabulary of approximately 50 words by 18 months of age, at which time he stopped adding words and lost the acquired vocabulary. He was diagnosed with moderate autism at age 2. His parents worked diligently addressing digestive and dietary concerns and chronic upper respiratory infections. At age 6 years, Jake continues to be nonverbal, using both a picture-based system (Picture Exchange Communication System) and an electronic communication device. He recently completed Pivotal Response Training (PRT), which resulted in increased attempts at verbalization; however, Jake is only able to produce approximations of three consonants and one vowel. He demonstrates behaviors associated with a significant childhood apraxia of speech, including groping of the articulators, severely limited and inconsistent productions, and notable oral sensory concerns including food texture preferences, and a need for nearly constant chewing. Jake attends a public school program allowing for maximum participation in the regular education classroom. He has one-on-one assistance to facilitate his performance in the regular education setting. His family has pursued dietary interventions, music therapy, and other alternative interventions to varying degrees of success. An organic diet and homeopathic supplements have resulted in a significant decrease in upper respiratory illnesses in Jake. Jake lives with his parents and 3-year-old sister; mom is an SLP and dad is a graphic artist.

Jean came to the clinic as a 5-year-old diagnosed with high functioning autism. She was readily verbal with several articulation errors noted, some of which were developmental in nature. She is currently a 7-year-old, fully included in the regular education setting with support from the school SLP. She has OT needs which are being met on a consultative basis. Jean continues to require significant adaptations to the regular education curriculum in order to be able to function without one-on-one assistance in the classroom. She is beginning to experience difficulty in the classroom as the focus is shifting to more abstract concepts. Jean is very verbal and outgoing. She has social deficits which include difficulty engaging in conversational turn taking and inappropriate proxemics. She is the daughter of a single mother who is a student, and also lives part-time with her maternal grandmother, a teacher, to facilitate school placement.

Hank came to the clinic as a 2½-year old with a diagnosis of mild autism. He was verbal, and able to engage in some conversational turn taking. His parents report having concerns about his development during the first year of life. He had difficulty sleeping and tolerating various formulas. He was delayed in speaking his first words. He maintained minimal eye contact. He was enrolled in a preschool group to address social-communication needs. He made significant progress in a short period of time. He was able to ask and answer questions and make easy transitions within the group. Of particular interest was Hank's response to the use of a timer to help with transitions. Hank became overly conscious of the digital timer, preferring to watch the numbers change on the LED dial. A simple, wind-up egg timer was much more effective, and so was a silent timer that simply displays a colored area, usually red, until the time runs out. On his most recent birthday, Hank's mother proclaimed him "king for a day." But Hank said he could not be king, "because he was a boy, not a king." So, instead he was a "special boy" for the day. For his birthday snack at school, he decided not to bring cupcakes. Instead, he wanted to bring toaster tarts, brown-sugar cinnamon flavor. This is his all-time favorite snack, ever since finding it at the snack machine in our clinic building. He recently started gymnastics lessons and is playing soccer. Hank currently demonstrates high functioning autism. He lives with his parents (Ph.D. faculty), a 6-year-old sister, and 3-year-old twin brothers. His siblings do not appear to demonstrate behaviors associated with autism.

Lisa was referred to the clinic by her mother at the age of 2 years because of significant communication deficits. Lisa was essentially nonverbal, screaming and crying as her primary means of communication. Her mother reported being concerned about Lisa at 2 months of age when Lisa failed to demonstrate a social smile. The mother was told by the pediatrician not to be concerned. By 1 year of age, Lisa was not responding to her name. She did not produce words prior to her second birthday. She was enrolled in a preschool language development group structured to emulate a center-based preschool program. She did not tolerate transitions well, although if allowed to join the group after an activity had begun, she would often participate with enthusiasm. After several months in the program, she was referred for further assessment and received a diagnosis of moderate autism. Lisa made significant progress over approximately 24 months, following treatment with antifungal medications and dietary modifications. At age 4, Lisa was demonstrating language production skills commensurate with her age level. Lisa is the second of three daughters, living with her parents. Her older sister demonstrated notable difficulties with hyperlexia, conversational management, and pragmatics skills suggesting that she might be demonstrating a milder form of autism spectrum disorder relative to Lisa. The youngest child was provided with an organic diet while in utero and following birth. She did not demonstrate any behaviors associated with autism at age 2 years.

❖ Discussion Starters ❖

1. What do the children included in the case studies have in common? How do they differ?

2. Describe persons you have encountered who have autism. How are they similar or different from the children included in the case studies?

Chapter 3

Asperger Syndrome:
A Potato on the Couch

Key Concepts

❖ Cognitive Abilities
   Memory
   Flexibility
   Executive Function

❖ Language Abilities
   Figurative Language
   Paralinguistic Skills
   Pedantic Speech
   Verbal Fluency

❖ Social Abilities

❖ Sensory and Motor Skills

❖ Academic Skills
   Hyperlexia
   Narrative Development
   Scoring of Narratives
   Writing

❖ Asperger Syndrome ❖

Children with Asperger syndrome are a fascinating population. Children with Asperger syndrome demonstrate normal cognitive skills, while often presenting with significant academic challenges. The academic challenges can be the result of a learning difficulty or idiosyncrasies within the child (Myles & Simpson, 2003). Children with Asperger syndrome do not demonstrate early deficits in language form (syntax, phonology) and language content (semantics); however, the use of language (pragmatics) is compromised and interferes with social development. Wing (1998, as cited in Attwood, 1998) stated that persons with Asperger syndrome "perceive [that] the world makes sense to them and has some aspects that are admirable, but it often brings them into conflict with conventional ways of thinking, feeling and behaving . . . (they) need help in finding ways of adapting to the world as it is in order to use their skills constructively" (p. 9).

Although Donna Williams has a diagnosis of autism, she is noted to have high functioning autism, and so has a great deal in common with those who have Asperger syndrome. She lists challenges that she has encountered and they are relevant to those with Asperger syndrome. She notes that she lacks (a) a connectedness to her body and feelings, (b) friendships in which she feels equal, (c) an understanding of when to give up and who to give up on, (d) an acceptance of the world without guarantees, and (e) a knowledge of the future (Williams, 1994).

As the cause of Asperger syndrome is not known, we will not speculate here. However, boys are affected more than girls, pointing to some underlying genetic component. Asperger syndrome does tend to run in families, often with a parent (most often the father) demonstrating Asperger syndrome or aspects of the syndrome. Additionally, there may be extended family members with autism. Several disorders are also seen in extended family members including depression, bipolar disorder, dyslexia, and dyspraxia (Myles & Simpson, 2003). What can differentiate Asperger syndrome from autism is the narrow interest in often unusual topics. Children with autism tend to develop intense focus on objects or just parts of objects.

❖ Cognitive Abilities ❖

The cognitive abilities of children with Asperger syndrome are, by definition, at or above average. However, measuring the IQ of a child with Asperger syndrome with a language-heavy assessment tool may result in an underestimation of cognitive skills. It is essential that an intelligence test that is language-free be used to fully assess learning and cognitive potential. Several test tools are available for this type of assessment, including the Leiter International Performance Scale-Revised (LIPS-R) (Roid & Miller, 2002), the Universal Nonverbal Intelligence Test (UNIT) (Bracken & McCallum, 2002), and for a brief screening tool, the Test of Nonverbal Intelligence-3rd edition (TONI-3) (Brown, Sherbenou, & Johnsen, 2000) can be useful.

Children with Asperger syndrome tend to demonstrate a relative strength in memory skills. While they do have excellent visual memory (often photographic), some with Asperger syndrome can demonstrate superior auditory memory skills as well, recalling entire movie scripts, verbatim. One young adult, Chandler, reported that while he could remember virtually anything he read or saw, he could not recall conversational exchanges. He needed to take copious notes during conversations in order to be able to recall the content of the conversation later. During our initial meetings, Chandler did not write notes as he did not want to appear different or odd. He would leave the meeting, go home, and e-mail us to ask for a reiteration of what had transpired from our meeting and to clarify future plans for follow-up appointments, further assessments, and the like, even though he assured us that he understood everything discussed prior to leaving the meeting. Once he felt safe enough to expose his needs, Chandler began to take notes in all meetings; however, his handwriting was labored, slow, and often illegible. He was given a pocket PC and collapsible keyboard as part of a research project. He typed all his notes with great speed and accuracy. He has excellent keyboarding skills as he can visualize the keyboard, and types approximately 90 words per minute with no errors.

Cognitive flexibility is often problematic for the child with Asperger syndrome. There is a tendency for rigid thinking, thinking in absolutes, which contributes to the difficulty seen in dealing with failure or change. For the child with Asperger syndrome, failure is the opposite of winning only. There may be no concept of trying hard and not being successful. There may be no understanding of the concept of luck. Consequently, those with Asperger syndrome are often not graceful losers during game play. The resulting "meltdown" associated with losing will likely further alienate the child's peers. Inflexible thinking can also have an impact with regard to learning from the consequences of one's behavior. The child with Asperger syndrome may not recognize that his strategy for solving a problem has failed. He may not seek help in determining another strategy without direct instruction and cueing from teachers, parents, and even peers. Being wrong can be particularly difficult for the child with Asperger syndrome. While the child may, in fact, be wrong about something, he will not recognize that and most attempts to sway his thinking will result in an argument or power struggle that may not be worth it. In other words, just agree to disagree and move on. Along the same lines, the concept of practicing a skill as one does in the classroom is often frustrating for the person with Asperger syndrome. Once the task has been completed correctly, the person with Asperger syndrome may not see any reason to repeat the task. Once it is done, it is done.

Additionally, it is essential to consider learning style and executive functions when addressing the needs of children with Asperger syndrome. Assessing the learning style allows us to make better treatment recommendations for children with Asperger syndrome. Knowing about how the child learns, where, and when are important when intervening (Kaufman & Lord Larson, 2005). Children with Asperger syndrome often prefer to learn alone, and to focus on topics of their choosing. This makes participation in the regular classroom activities challenging as group work and curriculum-determined topics prevail in the public school setting.

Executive functioning is often challenging for the child with Asperger syndrome. Executive functions of concern include planning, organizing, and carrying out events, setting priorities, task completion, successful multitasking. A large number of classroom tasks include these challenges to executive functions. Therefore, the assessment of executive function and the recognition of its impact on the academic performance of children with Asperger syndrome are essential for success in the classroom. If you are not sure what is meant by executive function with regard to organization, look in the desk of a child with Asperger syndrome. Often, you will find papers that were to be turned in the week before. You may find 15 pencils when the child reported not having one for class work. The book bag of the child with Asperger syndrome can also be terribly disorganized and lost items may be found, lost work recovered. Organizational strategies will be discussed in Chapter 5.

The literature is divided over whether children with Asperger syndrome have the same problems with theory of mind as those with autism. Some studies have shown theory of mind deficits while others have not. Watters (2005) found that 37% of the children with Asperger syndrome sampled were not able to complete a second-order false belief task. This type of task requires that the child report what one character thinks that another character thinks about an event. This difference was not explained by language or memory concerns. Knowing that theory of mind impacts learning, thinking, and communication skills, this area needs further investigation so that effective teaching and treatment strategies can be developed.

❖ Language Abilities ❖

Children with Asperger syndrome are described in the DSM-IV (2000) as having no early language delays. It is important to recall that while children with Asperger syndrome may produce complete and syntactically correct utterance with an impressive vocabulary, they show difficulties with the pragmatic aspects of language use early on. A common misconception regarding the language skills of children with Asperger syndrome is that they do not present with language difficulties; however, the diagnostic criteria for diagnosis only state that there is no "general delay in language." Therefore, one can expect to encounter language deficits in the child with Asperger syndrome, particularly as the child grows older. The deficits seen may include problems with the comprehension of abstract concepts, and figurative language (metaphors, idioms, humor, and sarcasm).

Problems with the understanding and use of nonverbal communication are also noted in the child with Asperger syndrome. For example, the child with Asperger syndrome may stand too close and speak too loudly. The child may stare at another or make little eye contact. The child with Asperger syndrome may present with a flat affect, often mistaken for disinterest or boredom. This affect difference can be misinterpreted by the classroom teacher as a lack of cooperation or enthusiasm. The bottom line is that all of these behaviors serve to further separate children with Asperger syndrome from their peers.

Difficulties with the effective use of language or pragmatics are usually evident early on. These difficulties may take the form of lectures from the child on a topic of interest to them. Children with Asperger syndrome have been noted to walk up to strangers and launch into explanations regarding the weather, planets, or some historical figure of interest. In addition to the unusual nature of the topics of interest, children with Asperger syndrome may not introduce themselves prior to beginning their verbal dissertation. All of these pragmatic oddities serve to draw attention, rarely positive, to the child, and may further serve to contribute to their social isolation. Children with Asperger syndrome have problems with conversational skills including repairing a conversational breakdown, shifting topics, and including seemingly irrelevant information in the conversation. Long pauses may occur during the conversation while the person with Asperger syndrome seeks to think about and formulate a response. Most of us make a comment to the effect that we are thinking, thereby letting our partner know we are still involved in the conversation. This is not a strategy usually used by the person with Asperger syndrome. Some children with Asperger syndrome have a learned response to any question, that being "I don't know," while others do not respond at all. This leaves the communication partner unsure of how to proceed.

The person with Asperger syndrome is also often known as "the little professor." This is related to the use of pedantic speech patterns, in addition to often vast knowledge of a variety of topics. Pedantic speech refers to the overly formal way some with Asperger syndrome speak, even in a casual conversation. For example, contractions are an accepted part of casual speaking. Some children with Asperger syndrome do not use contractions, causing them to sound more formal than their peers. Chandler, a 22-year-old with Asperger syndrome, speaks in a somewhat formal fashion, but his e-mail messages are extremely formal and verbose. Contractions are rare and slang is never used. He formulates messages that are paragraphs in length. This has also been observed in Renee, a 19-year-old female with Asperger syndrome.

Chandler and Renee also have problems with verbal fluency. Both tend to produce part and whole word repetitions, as well as numerous incomplete utterances and a high rate of revisions and verbal fillers (*um, uh*). Both report high levels of anxiety associated with speaking to others and report this anxiety contributes to their decreased fluency. Chandler was evaluated and was found to be mildly dysfluent in conversation, but had no dysfluencies when reading. He reported great anxiety related to using the phone, and initially refused to share his phone number, requesting all communication be in the form of e-mail. Renee was noted to speak at a very fast rate, and this seemed to contribute to her lack of verbal fluency.

Perhaps Donna Williams (1994) stated it best. She wrote, "I have language like a one-hundred-year old (the best possible), but I have the social communication skills of a badly trained young child. I can talk on many topics but when being social and language come together, they drag my level of functioning way down" (p. 123).

❖ Social Abilities ❖

Children with Asperger syndrome can be socially withdrawn or socially outgoing. This variability can result in confusion if one expects all children with Asperger syndrome to be aloof or isolated. It should be noted however, that those who are outgoing are often plagued with social deficits. They may be described as socially stiff or awkward, inflexible, self-centered, and unable to read nonverbal cues (Myles & Simpson, 2003). As a result of the lack of awareness of social rules and etiquette, children with Asperger syndrome can remain socially isolated while actively desiring social interaction. Furthermore, children with Asperger syndrome may engage in inappropriate behaviors that result from their inability to predict outcomes. A child with Asperger syndrome may appear to lash out aggressively, but this acting out is less about being aggressive toward another, and more about self-protection. When one cannot effectively predict outcomes or generalize learning from one context to another, or when one becomes stressed and overwhelmed by the real world, self-protection and withdrawal are to be expected.

One aspect of the social difficulties experienced by children with Asperger syndrome that must be discussed and understood is their response to authority. In our experience, most of the children with Asperger syndrome we have treated tend to view adults as peers. They do not seem to make distinctions based on age and position as others do. They will engage in a debate or discussion with adults when their typically developing peers would not. Some children with Asperger syndrome have a very hard time if confronted by an adult, and may become more stubborn and rigid in response to that confrontation. Their behavior in response to the adult may rapidly escalate to the point of anger, and in some cases can become physical. This does not mean that the child may physically attack the adult, but may throw objects or destroy items. There is no evidence children with Asperger syndrome are any more aggressive than the next child; however, reports of children with Asperger syndrome being aggressive are relatively common. This appears to occur when the demands of the situation exceed the social and communication abilities of the child with Asperger syndrome. The social and communication deficits paired with limited tolerance for frustration can result in aberrant physical responses.

As children with Asperger syndrome grow older, they can develop skill at engaging the adult in power struggles. We as adults like to be heard and acknowledged when we believe we are correct. This is true of the child and teen with Asperger syndrome. We as adults have to be willing *not* to be engaged in a power struggle. We have to be willing *not* to be heard. Persons with Asperger syndrome can be tenacious in their ability to argue and debate. What starts as a simple discussion can easily escalate into a serious but unproductive confrontation. Finally, punitive measures do not generally work well with children with Asperger syndrome and the focus needs to be on increasing skills and abilities so that problems can be avoided.

❖ Sensory and Motor Skills ❖

Children with Asperger syndrome can demonstrate sensory issues similar to those of children with autism. Difficulties with touch, noise, and other sensory stimuli have been noted in persons with Asperger syndrome. It is not apparent if those with Asperger syndrome have better or worse responses to sensory stimuli. It is likely that, as with many issues related to autism and Asperger syndrome, the responses vary from individual to individual.

Anecdotal information indicates that children with Asperger syndrome have gross and fine motor concerns. However, these are not universal observations and the nature of the motor deficits can vary significantly from child to child. Wing (1981) noted the potential for clumsiness and that has been confirmed by a few studies (Smith, 2000; Smith & Bryson, 1994). Manjiviona and Prior (1995) reported that children with Asperger syndrome learned to walk a few months after expected. The skills that can be affected in the child with Asperger syndrome can include walking and running (an odd gait is often noted), throwing and catching a ball (pointing to eye-hand coordination problems), and balance. Given the social nature of play, the physical limitations demonstrated by children with Asperger syndrome further serve to isolate them from peers. It is during game play that social and communication skills are often refined and certainly practiced. If the child with Asperger syndrome is not able to manage the motor task, there is little chance for him to benefit from the social-communication practice.

In general, children with Asperger syndrome are often described as clumsy and awkward. Children with Asperger syndrome are often limited in athletic ability, lacking the gross motor coordination to be successful at sports. If that is the case, efforts should be made to allow the child to participate at a level where he can succeed. Children with Asperger syndrome can be great equipment managers and score keepers. This allows participation without the potential embarrassment that can come from group sports. Parents are encouraged however to enroll their child with Asperger syndrome in a variety of physical activities as early as possible. While no studies have confirmed this, it seems that those who participate in physical activities earlier seem to have slightly better skills as they grow up.

With regard to fine motor skills, children with Asperger syndrome can demonstrate significant challenges, both in self-help skills, including buttoning and tying, and in the classroom, specifically with handwriting, drawing, and scissor use. Many children with Asperger syndrome present handwriting that is large and unwieldy with regard to lined paper. They can have great difficulty writing small enough to fit onto typical lined paper. Others with Asperger syndrome can produce extremely accurate letter production, but at a great cognitive and physical cost. These children often have a high degree of perfectionism relative to writing and will labor to produce each letter *a* exactly the same way every time. This can result in numerous erasures. If the repeated erasures damage the paper, an outburst may follow.

The cognitive, physical, and emotional price the child with Asperger syndrome may pay for motor concerns should not exceed the costs of the task. For example, a child with Asperger syndrome whom we treated had odd letter formation when writing the letter *r*. He was simply not able to write those letters correctly when under any kind of pressure (time limits). Consequently, he had serious challenges when faced with spelling tests. He would spell the words on the test correctly with his unusual letter formation and would then be marked wrong. He repeatedly told his teacher that he could not make the letter another way and that he had indeed spelled the words correctly. He was not given credit for his answers, and he became extremely frustrated. Eventually he began acting out right before the spelling tests. The question posed to the teacher was whether she was assessing his spelling or handwriting and that with his motor issues, she might consider allowing him to type his answers on the class computer. She agreed and his spelling grades soared to 100% and his behavior improved dramatically.

❖ Academic Skills ❖

The best predictor of the academic success of a child with Asperger syndrome may be whether the subject matter is of interest to the child. Many children with Asperger syndrome enjoy science and history classes. Both are fact driven subjects, playing to the strengths of many with Asperger syndrome. Language arts and English classes can sometimes pose problems for children with Asperger syndrome. These classes can involve figurative language, multiple meanings for words, and creative writing, all of which can be a challenge for children with Asperger syndrome. Motivation is key to the academic success of children with Asperger syndrome.

In fact, motivation is probably, in and of itself, the most challenging aspect of Asperger syndrome. Children with Asperger syndrome are motivated most often by subjects, often extremely narrow topics, of their own choosing. How one might translate that interest into academic success should be the objective of the teacher, therapist, and parent. Some children will complete less desired academic tasks when rewarded with the free pursuit of favorite topics. Many children served in our center work under contracts which they help draft. The child agrees to complete school work with a minimum of protest with the promise of time to pursue special interests. Others with Asperger syndrome may benefit from having the curricular objectives placed in the context of a favored topic. Temple Grandin, a person with high functioning autism, encourages teachers to use the focused interests as the teaching context. If the child is interested in trains, use that interest to address academic goals and objectives. For example, at a recent teacher training workshop, a participant noted that a child with whom he worked loved trains and only wanted to talk about and play with trains. It was noted that trains could be used as a reinforcer for completing conventional class work or that the work could be adapted using a train theme. If you need to practice counting, count train cars. If you need to master sequencing, build a train in a specific sequence (engine, coal car, and caboose).

One school of thought is that some children with Asperger syndrome have concomitant learning disabilities. Asperger (1944) noted the uneven academic performance of the children with whom he worked. Frith (1991) and Siegel, Minshew, and Goldstein (1996) described learning profiles in children with Asperger syndrome that are similar to those of children with learning disabilities. Certainly the challenges faced by children with Asperger syndrome could be expected to contribute to learning difficulties. It is reported that children with Asperger syndrome have problems understanding abstract concepts, metaphor, idioms, and other forms of figurative language, while a relative strength is noted in the comprehension and storage of fact-based classroom subjects. Griswold, Barnhill, Myles, Hagiwara, and Simpson (2002) found that children with Asperger syndrome had average academic achievement scores overall and strengths in oral expression and reading recognition, but specific weaknesses were noted in listening comprehension and written language. Problems were also noted in solving mathematical equations. The difficulty noted with this aspect of mathematics is the shifting value of X. If X = 3, then how can it equal 7? It is the nature of Asperger syndrome and the need for absolutes that impacts the child's learning in this arena.

Reading. Reading skills have been examined in children with Asperger syndrome. There appears to be a fair level of variability among those with Asperger syndrome in this regard. Some children with Asperger syndrome demonstrate hyperlexia and well-developed word recognition skills along with poor comprehension, but others seem to struggle with reading and lag behind their typical peers in cracking the code (Attwood, 1998). While it has been accepted that children with Asperger syndrome are able to recognize words, the thought was that they were fairly adept at word decoding. An ongoing study at our center has yielded preliminary data that would indicate that some children with Asperger syndrome are relying on a large sight word vocabulary to read words and are not using sound-symbol associations to decode words; therefore, an assessment of the child's phonics skills is indicated. It is vital that the child's independent reading level be established, that is, the level at which he can read with over 98–100% accuracy with 90–100% comprehension. One must also determine the child's instructional reading level, which is defined as the level at which he can recognize words with 95% accuracy with comprehension at 75% or better (Sundbye, 2001). A miscue analysis during oral reading is also an important assessment, examining the error patterns of the reader in passages. Errors to be examined in this analysis include the graphic similarity between the target and error, class substitutions, and the number of self-corrections (Stanford & Siders, 2001).

While the focus has generally been on the oral reading skills of children with Asperger syndrome, it is important that their ability to listen to material being read aloud also be assessed. Aiming for 75% comprehension or better, the examiner reads aloud at a level above the child's instructional reading level. When the comprehension falls below 75%, the listening capacity has been determined. This skill is important for successful learning in the classroom, especially during lecture-based instruction.

Grandin (1984) noted that she spends her time reading but that her "interests are factual and my recreational reading consists mostly of science and livestock publications. I have little interest in novels with complicated interpersonal relationships, because I am

unable to remember the sequence of events" (p. 152). This is com-
pelling information coming from a woman with high functioning
autism who has successfully completed a Ph.D. and is on faculty at
a major university.

Writing. Writing for children with Asperger syndrome can be a
challenge or strength. For many children with Asperger syndrome,
it is the physical act of writing that impairs their ability to produce
written work. While the child may not have specific fine motor
deficits, handwriting requires a cognitive effort above and beyond
the formation of what will be written. The child with Asperger syndrome who demonstrates perfectionism may refuse to pick up the
pencil and begin an activity simply to avoid having to make every
letter perfectly. Barring motoric problems, the child with Asperger
syndrome should be evaluated to determine how well he or she is
able to research a topic, organize the research, write for an audi-
ence, craft an outline, and create and edit drafts. Writing becomes
a more demanding task as the child with Asperger syndrome moves
up through late elementary and middle school. Note taking requires
a great deal of attention, rapid processing of language, and adequate
fine motor skill to write quickly. Sachs (1995) noted that when
reading work by Temple Grandin (an extraordinary person with
high functioning autism) one is struck by "peculiar narrative gaps
and discontinuities, sudden perplexing changes of topic brought
about by Temple's failure to appreciate that her reader does not
share the important background information that she possesses. In
more general terms, autistic writers seem to get 'out of tune' with
their readers, fail to realize their own or their readers' states of
mind" (p. 253).

Narrative Skills. Narrative discourse has been shown to be an
excellent predictor of academic success. As noted, reading comprehension is compromised and this is due, at least in part, to the child
not recognizing the structure of narratives. Given that, the production of coherent, cohesive narratives may be deficient as well. The
direct and explicit instruction in the use of story grammar is likely
to help the student produce meaningful written work. *Story grammar* refers to the structure or framework of a narrative. Aspects of
story grammar include setting, initiating event, internal response,
plan, attempt, consequence, and reaction (Johnston, 1982). Several

story grammar scoring schemes are available to support these activities. Applebee's approach (Klecan-Aker & Kelty, 1990) can be useful as a representation of the stages of narrative development. Narrative stages include heap stories, sequence stories, primitive narratives, chain narratives, and true narratives. Heap stories are usually produced by age 2 and include labels and descriptions of actions without a central theme. Sequence stories, observed by age 3, have a central theme or character around which events are named. Primitive narratives contain three aspects of story grammar, an initiating event, an action, and a consequence and are noted by 4½ years of age. Chain narratives emerge by age 5 and have a weak plot and four story grammar elements, including the three from the primitive narrative, as well as a plan. Finally, true narratives include all aspects of story grammar, and are produced by most children by age 7. Several visual supports are available to facilitate the development of this skill set. These usually include visual representations of all aspects of story grammar. Once a child is able to create a cohesive, oral narrative, the creation of written narratives can be addressed.

Another problem that can arise when the child with Asperger syndrome is writing is *unintentional plagiarism*. As discussed, many children with Asperger syndrome have excellent recall of things they have heard or read. Therefore, when asked to write about a particular topic, the child with Asperger syndrome may recall material verbatim. As a result of the concomitant language difficulties associated with Asperger syndrome, the child may have great difficulty with the concept of paraphrasing material. With explicit instruction and support, it may be expected that the child will be able to develop in the area. Little research has examined this aspect of the syndrome.

The following situations that include Jerry and Trent, while amusing, illustrate the cognitive, social, and linguistic deficits that can be found in children with Asperger syndrome (Stewart, 2004).

Jerry and his family went to Burger King to eat and to play in the balls. Jerry and his brother were playing in the balls when another child came in with a toy from his meal. Jerry began screaming at the child, "you are breaking the rules, there are no toys allowed in the balls!" Jerry's mother called him over to explain that the boy was only 2 years old and he probably didn't understand the rules and to let his parents take care of him. While they were talking, the boy lost his toy in the balls and his mother climbed in the balls to help him find it. When Jerry saw this, he became very belligerent and began yelling at the mother, "You are not supposed to be in the balls, it is against the rules!" Jerry's mother tried to explain that she was just helping her child find his toy and that it was okay. This was not enough for Jerry. He proceeded to pick up the rule sign, which was large, and take it over to the mother, who was still in the balls, and point at the sign saying, "the rule sign says, no adults in the balls!"

Jerry enjoys reading the Discovery Kids Magazine. In one issue about the sun, he read that you should not look directly into the sun because it could blind you. (I think we have all heard our parents say that at least once!) Soon after reading that article Jerry visited a pumpkin patch and had his face painted by a vendor. A nice lady approached Jerry and asked him what he had painted on his face, Jerry said "Virginia Tech, and do not look directly into the sun or it will blind you." The nice lady gave him a strange look and walked away.

When Jerry was old enough, his mother taught him how to run his own bath water. She told him to make sure that it was not too hot and not to fill the tub up too high because it could run over or he could drown. While Jerry was bathing one night, his mother walked in to see only an inch of water in the tub. She said, "Jerry, why is there only a little bit of water in the tub?" He replied, "Well Mom, you said not to fill up the tub too high so I only put a little bit of water in."

Jerry and his mother were putting their shoes on to walk to the mailbox. As they were walking out of the door, his mother said, "Let's hit the road!" Jerry stopped, looked at his mother, looked at the road, and firmly stated, "Mom, if we hit the road it would hurt us because the road is hard."

Jerry's aunt came to his house one day to wish him luck for an upcoming school project. She said, "Jerry, I'll be thinking about you tomorrow, break a leg!" He looked at her in a state of shock and replied, "You really should not say things like that. That was not very nice!"

Jerry was having a birthday party, so his mother decorated appropriately with helium balloons and streamers. The next morning, noticing that the balloons were no longer floating, Jerry's mother said, "Oh no, look what happened, Jerry!" He replied, "It is alright, Mom, they were filled with helium and helium is a gas and has escaped. That is what happened, the helium escaped and left the air and that is why the balloons are not floating anymore." "Thanks for the science lesson, son," his mother replied. "You're welcome!" Jerry said.

When Jerry enters "his world" he sometimes holds his arms out and flaps them around while dancing in circles. His mother commented that he looked like a butterfly floating around. He replied factually, "I am not a butterfly. I am a human. Butterflies are insects and have wings, humans do not, and that is why I am a human."

Jerry has difficulty explaining his emotions and feelings. One time when he was very sick and running a fever, his mother asked him "How do you feel, Jerry?" He looked at his mother very strangely then began looking and touching his skin. He said, "Mom, my skin feels the same as it always does. It is still smooth."

One day after school, Jerry was talking about a kid in his classroom "looking a little different". His mother was trying to decipher Jerry's code so she asked him, "Jerry, is this kid a black person?" Jerry looked at his Mom like she was crazy and said, "No Mom, his skin is not black, it was a dark brown color. Everyone has the same skin as you and I do, some people's skin is brown, some light brown, and some dark brown, but we are all the same, just different shades of brown." Jerry's mother had just finished pumping gas and gave Jerry the money to pay the attendant. When the attendant came to the window, Jerry handed her the money and she said, "Thank you, you are a good helper. Who are those friends in the back seat there?" Jerry replied factually, "that boy right there is my little brother, and that brown boy, well he is my cousin."

During a family reunion, Trent was standing on the porch and asked his uncle, "Can I go to the bathroom?" His uncle said yes, and Trent proceeded to drop his pants in front of everyone. He was stopped just in time, but was totally confused as to why his uncle gave him permission to go and then got upset when he did.

Trent once had a pair of Elmo shoes that were his favorite to wear. One day he put them on the wrong feet. Knowing that if you tell Trent that his shoes were on the 'wrong feet' that he would go look for the other feet to put them on, his mother told him that Elmo goes on the outside. Trent looked down at his shoes, looked up tearfully at his mother and said "But it's cold outside".

Trent was riding in the back seat of the car, with his grandparents, when his grandfather removed his hat. Trent looked at his grandfather's head in shock; apparently he had never realized that his grandfather had no hair. He looked over at his grandmother and asked, "What happened to Grandpa's hair?" "Oh he lost it," she replied. Trent immediately bent over and started looking around in the car floor trying to find it.

Trent had a relative who worked at his school as a secretary. She would fill in the family on Trent's behavior every day after school. One day, she told his cousin that Trent got in trouble for talking during silent lunch. His cousin decided to test Trent's honesty and asked him how his day had gone.

"Okay," Trent said.

"Did you get in trouble?" his cousin asked.

"No, . . . umm . . . let me think . . . yes."

"Well, what happened?"

"Umm, we were in the cafeteria and there were these kids at the far table near the stage, they were talking and being really loud and disrespectful and I was one of them."

Trent had an upset stomach and was feeling pretty bad. He told his cousin that he was thirsty, so he gave him ginger ale and told him to sip it slowly to keep it from upsetting his stomach. He looked a little confused at first and then appeared to understand.

"Oh yeah, we don't want to upset my stomach, we want it to be happy . . . right?"

His cousin pondered explaining it further, but instead he said, "Yeah, that's right."

Trent's cousin wasn't feeling well and decided to go to bed early. It was close to Trent's bedtime so he told Trent goodnight and asked him not to wake him up unless it was something important. After about 7 minutes, Trent knocked on his door and started calling for his cousin. His cousin jumped up, rushed to the door, and opened it to find Trent standing there looking calm and content. He said, "Do you know how old Thomas Jefferson would be if he were alive today?" His cousin replied, "Trent, I asked you not to wake me unless it was something important!" He said, "I thought that history *is* important!!"

A boy named Tyler was bullying Trent at school, so Trent decided to tell the teacher. The teacher talked with both students about the situation and decided to give Tyler the benefit of the doubt because it was Tyler's word against Trent's word. Another student overhead Tyler's continuous threats to Trent and told the teacher in Trent's defense. The teacher had a second talk with both students and decided to send Tyler to the principal. Trent came home and told his cousin what had happened, but he still seemed upset. His cousin asked him why he was upset and Trent replied, "Mrs. Turner said she gave Tyler the benefit of the doubt the first time and she didn't give me anything."

Trent's best friend Jerry (mentioned above) and his little brother came over to play with Trent one day. Trent was telling Jerry about a time when a friend, Jordan, came over to stay the night with him. He said, "Jordan doesn't have a TV and when he stayed with us, he only wanted to watch TV the whole time and wouldn't even play outside." Jerry had been learning about idioms with the speech therapist at school. He said, "He sounds like a potato on the couch . . . that's what is called an idiom."

One day Trent was talking about becoming President of the United States and listing off all of the things he would do if he became President. He quickly decided not to have an office because he remembered reading that many of our presidents 'died in office'.

Trent's granddad became ill at work and had to go home early. The next day, Trent and his granddad met some of his co-workers for lunch. His co-workers asked him why he had to leave early from work yesterday. He said, "Well, I started getting sick, and I thought that I could keep working, but then I lost my cookies." Trent replied, "I bet Sassy (his dog) ate them."

❖ Case Studies ❖

Aaron was referred to the clinic at age 9 years with a diagnosis of oppositional defiant disorder and attention deficit disorder. He was noted to be very verbal and sarcastic. He participated in a study of theory of mind, and was noted to respond as those with high functioning autism and Asperger syndrome in that he was unable to take another's perspective to successfully complete the tasks. He received a diagnosis of Asperger syndrome. He developed an alter ego named Kitty who only interacted with his mother and sister. Kitty asked questions regarding why social skills were important. Kitty asked all the questions that Aaron could not bring himself to ask, as he was not able to acknowledge that he had any difficulties. Through Kitty, Aaron received the answers and information he needed to begin to accept his differences and to begin to integrate the social skills addressed in treatment. Following 2 years of participation in group intervention, Aaron graduated from treatment. He is consistently named to the honor roll in middle school. He lives with his divorced mother and younger sister.

Joe was referred to the clinic following diagnosis of Asperger syndrome. At the age of 10 years, he was noted to be extremely verbal, able to discuss a wide range of topics, but he had difficulty engaging in a reciprocal conversation. Joe was outgoing, greeting adults with hugs, and he treated other children with respect and politeness. He tended to lecture others on his topics of interest which were numerous and varied (satellite phone transmission, Abraham Lincoln). Joe would find a topic of interest and would consume all forms of media regarding the topic including television, Internet, and print media. Joe was enrolled in group intervention for a period of approximately 2 years where conversational skills and group problem solving were targeted. Joe lives with his divorced mother and younger brother, who demonstrated significant symptoms of attention deficit hyperactivity disorder.

Seth, a 12-year-old, was referred to the center by his mother due to concerns regarding his need for social skill development. He had received a diagnosis of Asperger syndrome. Seth presented as a shy, aloof child with limited conversational skills. While it was apparent that he had a wealth of stored information, particularly with regard to sports, Seth had a difficult time sharing that information and reported that he did not like to talk. He was offered the opportunity to participate in preparation for his bar mitzvah, but he initially refused, citing his reluctance to speak in front of others. Following enrollment in a social skills group for approximately 1 year, Seth successfully completed his bar mitzvah. He continues to be a fully included honor roll student living with his parents and traveling extensively in the United States, Europe, and the Middle East.

Tony was referred to the clinic, at age 13 years, because of serious social-communication deficits, academic difficulties, and limited interests (Japanese anime, computers). He lived in a very rural area with limited resources available beyond the local school system Assessment revealed a normal nonverbal IQ with significant language processing deficits. A diagnosis of Asperger syndrome was made. He reported having great difficulty keeping track of his school work and getting to class with all necessary materials. He was provided with an organizational system to address his chronic problem of losing homework, pencils, etc. He lives with his parents and an older brother, who was noted to be academically gifted.

Chandler, age 22, wrote a 30-page self-assessment in a narrative format, with headings and subheadings. The document was outlined, topics were cross-referenced, and a reference list including works cited in the narrative as well as suggested readings completed it. Chandler sent his autobiography to me after a computer search matched my name with Asperger syndrome and local resources. His question was twofold, "What is wrong with me and can you help me?" In his paper, he recounted his childhood which saw him lacking in friends and exerting maximum effort to succeed academically. He struggled with an uncanny ability to decode any word, but an inability to comprehend books. He recalled being labeled as learning disabled but never receiving the type of help he needed to struggle less, the kind of help that would have made things just a little easier. He acted as the subject for two graduate theses, one targeting the use of a PDA for self-help and self-management skills, the other addressing his verbal dysfluencies. He participated in a peer support group for persons with Asperger syndrome on the local college campus, and is pursuing the completion of his bachelor's degree. He completed an associate degree in 1 year at the local community college.

❖ Discussion Starters ❖

1. What is most challenging with regard to educating those with Asperger syndrome?

2. Discuss someone you know who has Asperger syndrome.

3. What are the strengths and limitations associated with Asperger syndrome?

4. Brainstorm intervention strategies for those with Asperger syndrome.

5. Are high functioning autism and Asperger syndrome more alike than not?

Chapter 4

Assessment: Screening, Diagnosis, and Evaluation

Key Concepts

❖ Diagnosis and Assessment   ❖ Informal Assessment

❖ Screening   ❖ Diagnosis

❖ Diagnostic Tools

Fewer than 50% of children with autism demonstrate signs of the disorder at birth. More than half of children diagnosed with autism appear to follow a course of normal development before experiencing a significant cessation of development and a serious regression of acquired skills. The change in development usually occurs between 18 and 24 months of age (Pangborn & Baker, 2001). Children with Asperger syndrome may not be diagnosed until they begin to demonstrate difficulty with abstract thinking and social interaction and increased frustration. It is not unusual for the child with Asperger syndrome to be misdiagnosed with attention and behavior problems resulting in a delay in effective treatment and educational planning (Kaufman & Lord Larson, 2005).

❖ Diagnosis and Assessment ❖

The initial diagnostic process can be the most intimidating to the family and child. Teams which may include educators and medical and allied health professionals often assess the child over a period of several hours. The evaluation may include extensive interviewing of the parents. The child being assessed may be seen one on one by allied health personnel or in what is often called an arena assessment, where more than one assessor interacts with the child at the same time or are in the assessment room at the same time. The parents and child may be overwhelmed during this time. It is vital that the assessment be organized so as to obtain the best information with minimum stress to the family.

The cognitive performance associated with autism has been described as ranging from severe deficits to above average abilities. Certainly the accurate assessment of cognitive potential is problematic in many with autism. The nature of cognitive testing requires motivation and joint attention, both areas of concern for a person with autism. Many cognitive test tools are language-based, requiring effective language processing and production skills for successful completion. While there are nonverbal intelligence measures available and these should be used at every opportunity to measure cognition, nonverbal tests still require motivation and joint attention.

The problem with using standardized tests for the evaluation and assessment of children with autism is the paucity of tools actually standardized on those with autism. Additionally, the nature of this type of testing does not always allow for flexibility in administration, unduly penalizing those with autism. As a result, the reliability of such measures may be compromised. This type of assessment can be compromised because of the variability of performance from day to day, sometimes moment to moment, in those with autism. The person may become distracted or inattentive during the session. Since motivation is a huge part of successful performance in children with autism, the nature of standardized testing may limit motivation (Janzen, 2003).

❖ Screening for Autism ❖

To facilitate the effective initial assessment, one must choose assessment tools which will provide the type of information needed at that given time. There are a variety of screening and diagnostic tools available for evaluating the child with autism and Asperger syndrome. It is imperative that the tools chosen be valid and reliable. Several screening tools are available that are determined to be psychometrically sound. These include the Ages and Stages Questionnaire (Squires, Potter, & Bricker, 1999), the Parents' Evaluation of Developmental Status (Glascoe, 1997), and the Communication and Symbolic Behavior Scale Developmental Profile (CSBSDP) and the Infant Toddler Checklist (Wetherby & Prizant, 2002). All three measures approach 80% specificity (fewer false negatives) and sensitivity (fewer false positives) for identifying children with developmental delays (ASHA, 2006).

Following the use of a general screener, there are several autism-specific screening tools available. There is limited empirical support for the use of these tools due to the complex nature of the clinical investigation of very young children with autism. Health care workers and educational agencies have provided limited validation of these tools by utilizing them with children who have already been identified with developmental disabilities. Validation of these tools as general and autism-specific screeners is still necessary before they can be used on the general population (ASHA, 2006). The following autism-specific screening tools have been shown to have demonstrated sensitivity and selectivity in limited but promising psychometric review.

Modified Checklist for Autism in Toddlers (M-CHAT). The M-CHAT (Robins, Fein, Barton, & Green, 2001) is a modification of the Checklist for Autism in Toddlers (CHAT) developed by Baron-Cohen, Allen, and Gillberg (1992). The original version consisted of 9 items while the M-CHAT expanded upon the original 9 questions for a total of 23 parent-directed questions. It has not been fully validated for screening in the general population, but early results are promising in this regard. The M-CHAT is available in both English and Spanish versions.

Pervasive Developmental Disorders Screening Test, Second Edition (PDDST-II). Seigel (2004) developed the PDDST-II as a parent interview tool divided in three stages. No peer-reviewed literature is available currently, but the test shows promise with regard to sensitivity. Emerging specificity is noted by the author as well. The first stage of the PDDST-II is for use in the primary care setting. Stage 2 is to be used for differential diagnosis between such difficulties as autism and specific language delay and mental retardation. Stage 3 of the test is intended to provide a symptom severity level, and differentiate between autism and other pervasive developmental disorders.

Screening Test for Autism in Two-Year Olds (STAT). The STAT is the result of nearly 10 years of development (Stone, Coonrod, & Ousley, 2000; Stone, Coonrod, Turner, & Pozdol, 2004; Stone & Ousley, 1997). The STAT has been shown to demonstrate good reliability as well as concurrent validity with the clinical diagnostic criteria and the Autism Diagnostic Observation Schedule (ADOS; Lord, Rutter, DiLavore, & Risi, 1999). The test uses a 20-minute play session that includes 12 activities that tap into the areas of play, motor imitation, and nonverbal communication.

Systematic Observation of Red Flags (SORF). Wetherby et al. (2004) developed this observational rating of 29 "red flags" for autism. The observer can utilize a video sample recorded during the administration of the Communication and Symboic Behavior Scale—Developmental Profile (CSBS-DP). The data to support the use of the SORF are being collected, but preliminary data indicate strong sensitivity and selectivity. Some behaviors that, when observed, seem to be indicative of autism included lack of eye gaze, lack of response to name, lack of showing gesture, unusual prosody, and lack of shared attention and interest.

❖ Diagnostic Tools ❖

Autism Diagnostic Observation Scale (ADOS). Because of its strong psychometric performance, the ADOS (Lord et al., 1999) is one of the gold standard tools for diagnosis of autism when research is conducted. Made up of four modules, the ADOS measures communication, social reciprocity, play stereotypic behavior, restricted interests, and other unusual behaviors associated with autism. The ADOS has a high degree of sensitivity and specificity, but it is noted to underinclude those with higher verbal performance, and to overinclude those with mild MR (Lord & Corsello, 2005).

Autism Diagnostic Interview, Revised (ADI-R). Rutter, LeCouteur, and Lord (2003a) created this comprehensive parent interview tool that serves as the other gold standard for the diagnosis of autism for research purposes. The ADI-R consists of three subscales (communication, social reciprocity, and restricted-repetitive behaviors), and requires several hours for the complete administration, so while noted to be sensitive and specific, the ADI-R is not practical for most clinical applications.

Childhood Autism Rating Scale (CARS). The CARS (Schopler, Reichler, & Renner, 1988) is one of the first interview and observation tools created to diagnose autism. Each of 15 areas is rated on a seven-point scale to determine the degree to which the child's behavior deviates from normal. The CARS has been found to have excellent agreement with the DSM-IV (2000) criteria (Rellini, Tortolani, Trillo, Carbone, & Montecchi, 2004). It takes 15 minutes to administer after an extended observation period.

Gilliam Autism Rating Scale (GARS). The GARS (Gilliam, 1995) is a checklist developed to allow for diagnosis and a rating of the severity of autism. The 56-item scale is standardized with a mean of

100 and a standard deviation of 10. A quotient of 90 or above is noted to be indicative of a high risk of autism. The sensitivity and selectivity originally reported in the test manual have not been supported by a recent study. South et al. (2002) noted that the GARS only had 48% sensitivity in identifying children diagnosed with autism according to the DSM-IV (2000). A revision is reportedly underway.

With regard to the diagnosis of Asperger syndrome, at least three studies have questioned whether Asperger syndrome is a variant of autism or a separate and distinct disorder (Ghaziuddin & Mountain-Kimchi, 2004; MacIntosh & Dissanayake, 2004; Miller & Orzonoff, 2000). While group trends have been noted, individual variation is such that distinguishing between the two is challenging. As a result, there are far fewer assessment tools available to diagnose Asperger syndrome.

Asperger Syndrome Diagnostic Scale (ASDS). The ASDS (Myles, Bock, & Simpson, 2001) contains 50 items that address observable behaviors to be used with children between the ages of 5 and 18 years. Standard scores and percentile ranks can be determined. The scale includes subscales assessing language (9 items), social (13 items), maladaptive (11 items), cognitive (10 items), and sensorimotor (7 items) skills. The ASDS can be used to identify persons with Asperger syndrome, measure progress in treatment, identify treatment goals, and for research purposes (Myles, Bock, & Simpson, 2001). Evaluation of the ASDS by others has not been reported in the literature.

Gilliam Asperger Disorder Scale (GADS). Created by Gilliam in 2001, the GADS is a behavioral rating scale used to identify persons with Asperger syndrome. Thirty-two items are divided into four subscales addressing social interaction (10 items), restricted patterns of behavior (8 items), cognitive patterns (7 items), and pragmatic skills (7 items). Both standard scores and percentile ranks can be obtained from the conversion of raw scores. The scale was normed on 371 subjects with Asperger syndrome from 46 states, Canada, Great Britain, Mexico, Australia, and other countries (Gilliam, 2001). A review of the literature did not reveal evaluation of the GADS as a diagnostic tool.

With regard to psychoeducational testing, two tools have been standardized on persons with autism and may prove useful in the educational planning process.

Psychoeducational Profile, Third Revision (PEP-3). The PEP-3 was developed in 1990 at Division TEACCH by Schopler, Reicher, Bashford, Lansing, and Marcus. This tool is useful up to age 12 years. It included assessment of seven developmental areas with an accompanying pathology scale. The tool allows for extremely flexible administration to accommodate the needs of individuals with autism. The test tool is currently in its third revision.

Adolescent and Adult Psychoeducational Profile (AAPEP). Developed by Mesibov, Schopler, Schaffer, and Landrus in 1988 at Division TEACCH, the test includes three different scales to assess needs in three different settings. The tool included the direct assessment scale, home scale, and school/work scale.

For the assessment of adaptive behavior, two assessment tools are available. Both have applicability for the assessment of autism and Asperger syndrome.

Behavior Assessment System for Children (BASC). This tool was created by Reynolds and Kamphaus in 1992. It is used to assess the emotional and behavioral issues associated with autism and Asperger syndrome. It contains a parent rating scale, a teacher rating scale, and a self-assessment scale for the child. It is useful in the examination of activity level, conduct problems, aggression, anxiety, depression, withdrawal, attention, adaptability, leadership skills, and social skills. A study (Barnhill et al., 2000) found the BASC to be useful in treatment planning for children with Asperger syndrome.

Vineland Adaptive Behavior Scale (VABS). Created in 1984 by Sparrow, Balla, and Cicchetti, the VABS has been used to interview the parents or primary caregivers as well as the classroom teacher. The areas assessed include communication, daily living, socialization, and motor skills.

Table 4–1 includes a brief description of a number of screening, diagnostic, and assessment measures available for use with children and adults with autism and Asperger syndrome.

Table 4-1. Screening, Diagnostic, and Assessment Tools for Autism and Asperger Syndrome

Test	Age Range	Primary Areas	Form of Assessment
Adolescent and Adult Psychoeducational Profile (AAPEP)	Adolescent to adult	• Vocational placement • Community placement	Formal and informal assessment
Adolescent/Adult Sensory Profile	Adolescent to adult	• Sensory processing	Questionnaire
Ages & Stages Questionnaires: Social Emotional (ASQ:SE): A Parent Completed, Child Monitoring System for Social Emotional Behaviors	6–60 months	• Self-regulation • Compliance • Adaptive functioning • Autonomy • Affect • Interaction with people	Questionnaire
Analysis of Sensory Behavior Inventory, Revised Edition (ASBI-R)	All	• Sensory processing	
Asperger Syndrome Diagnostic Scale (ASDS)	5–18 years	• Asperger syndrome • Cognition • Maladaptive skills • Language • Social skills • Sensorimotor skills	Norm-reference screening

continues

Test	Age Range	Primary Areas	Form of Assessment
Assessment of Basic Language and Learning Skills (ABLLS)	All	• Visual performance • Imitation • Receptive and expressive language • Social interaction • Classroom and daily living skills	Criterion-reference assessment
Autism Diagnostic Interview, Revised (ADI-R)	Mental age >18 months	• Differentiates mental retardation (MR) from autism	Parent interview
Autism Diagnostic Observation Schedule (ADOS)	15 months–40 years	• Communication • Social interaction • Imaginative play skills • Administrators must attend a 2-day training workshop and use ADOS in research	Play assessment

Table 4–1. *continued*

Test	Age Range	Primary Areas	Form of Assessment
Autism Screening Instrument for Educational Planning, Second Edition (Asperger syndrome IEP-2)	18 months–adult	• Sensory • Relating • Body concept • Language • Social self-help domains • Vocal behavior • Interaction • Communication • Learning rate	Screening
Autism Screening Questionnaire (ASQ)	6–21 years	• Assesses symptoms of Asperger syndrome and other high functioning autism spectrum disorders (ASD)	Screening questionnaire
Behavior Assessment System for Children (BASC)	6–18 years	• Hyperactivity • Conduct • Aggression • Anxiety • Depression • Withdrawal • Attention	Parent rating scale Teacher rating scale Self-assessment

Test	Age Range	Primary Areas	Form of Assessment
Behavior Assessment System for Children (BASC) *continued*		• Adaptability • Leadership • Social skills	
Checklist for Autism in Toddlers (CHAT)	1½–2 years	• Identifies children at risk for autism and other pervasive developmental disorders (PDD)	Screening checklist questionnaire
Child Behavior Checklist for Ages 6–18 (CBCL/6-18)	6–18 years	• Behavioral/emotional problems • Aggressive behavior • Anxious/depressed • Attention problems • Rule breaking behavior • Social problems • Thought problems • Withdrawn/depressed	Parent interview
Childhood Autism Rating Scale (CARS)	2 years and older	• Distinguishes autism from MR	Standardized assessment

continues

Table 4–1. *continued*

Test	Age Range	Primary Areas	Form of Assessment
Communication and Symbolic Behavior Scales Developmental Profile (CSBS DP), First Normed Edition	Communication age 6–24 months Chronological age 6 months–6 years	• Emotion and eye gaze • Communication • Gestures • Sounds • Words • Understanding and object use • Distinguishes autism from other communication disorders	Norm-referenced assessment
Developmental Play Assessment (DPA) Instrument	Infant–preschool	• Play assessment developed for children with disabilities	Play assessment
Early Coping Inventory (ECI)	4–36 months	• Coping behaviors of infants and toddlers in everyday living situations • Sensorimotor • Organization • Reactive behavior • Self-initiated behavior	Observation assessment

Test	Age Range	Primary Areas	Form of Assessment
Evaluating Acquired Skills in Communication, Revised (EASIC-R)	3 months–8 years	• Semantics • Syntax • Morphology • Pragmatics • Designed to allow the examinee to respond via sign, verbalization, or alternative augmentative communication (AAC)	Informal inventory
Functional Emotional Assessment Scale for Infancy and Early Childhood (FEAS)	Birth–5 years	• Functional, emotional, and developmental levels • Assists in designing an individualized intervention plan	Criterion-referenced
Gilliam Asperger Disorder Scale (GADS)	3–21 years	• Designed for individuals who may have Asperger syndrome • Behavior problems • Discriminates individuals with Asperger syndrome from autism and other disorders	Norm-referenced assessment

continues

61

Table 4–1. *continued*

Test	Age Range	Primary Areas	Form of Assessment
Infant/Toddler Sensory Profile	Birth–3 years	• Sensory processing in everyday life • Available in English and Spanish	Caregiver questionnaire
Krug Asperger's Disorder Index (KADI)	6–21 years	• Distinguishes individuals with Asperger syndrome from those with high functioning autism	Norm-referenced assessment
Modified Checklist for Autism in Toddlers (M-CHAT)	18 months–2 years	• Designed to detect autism in young children	Parent-report checklist
Motivation Assessment Scale (MAS)	All	• Social attention • Tangible rewards • Escape/avoidance • Sensory feedback	Interview/observation assessment
Pervasive Developmental Disorder Screening Test-II (PDDST-II)	18–36 months	• Designed to screen for autism when concerns arise	Parent report

Test	Age Range	Primary Areas	Form of Assessment
Psychoeducational Profile, Third Revision (PEP-3)	Developmental age 1–7 years Chronological age 1–12 years	• Communication • Motor skills • Personal self-care • Maladaptive behaviors • Home observation	Standardized assessment/ observation assessment
Revised Behavior Summarized Evaluation Scale (BSE-R)	3–15 years	• Monitors progression of skills • Differentiates autism from other developmental disorders • Social interaction • Attention • Sensory disturbances • Imitation behavior • Emotional reactions • Communication processes	
Screening Tool for Autism in Two-Year-Olds (STAT)	2–3 years	• Play assessment • Distinguishes children at risk for autism from those with other developmental disorders	Screening

continues

Table 4-1. *continued*

Test	Age Range	Primary Areas	Form of Assessment
Sensory Profile	3–10 years	• Sensory processing	Caregiver questionnaire
Social Communication Questionnaire (SCQ)	Toddler to adult	• Behavior	
Temperament and Atypical Behavior Scale (TABS): Early Childhood Indicators of Developmental Dysfunction	11–71 months	• Critical temperament • Self-regulation • Provides intervention strategies to reduce problematic behaviors	Norm-referenced scale
Vineland Adaptive Behavior Scales (VABS), Classroom Edition	3–12 years, 11 months	• Adaptive and maladaptive behavior • Used to diagnose MR • Specifically designed to appraise adaptive behavior of children with autism and other PDD	Scale
Vineland Social-Emotional Childhood Scales (SEEC)	Birth–5 years	• Social-emotional skills • Daily living functioning • Interpersonal relationships • Play, leisure time, and coping skills	Parent report

While numerous standardized test tools are available for the assessment of language comprehension and production, to date none have data specific to those with autism and Asperger syndrome. However, several tools are recommended by previous reviews (Bligh, cited in Michael Thompson Productions, 2000; Myles & Adreon, 2001) and based on our clinical experiences.

Language Processing Test—3 (LPT-3). Richard and Hanner (2005) produced the third version of the Language Processing Test. The test measures the ability to "match increasingly more meaning to information received and then formulate an expressive response." The LPT-3 begins with a simple naming task with each successive subtest requiring the processing (comprehension and response formulation) of increasingly complex information. The test has two pretests (labeling and stating functions) followed by six subtests, association, categorization, similarities, differences, multiple meanings, and attributes. The age range for this measure is 5 through 12 years.

Test for the Auditory Comprehension of Language—3 (TACL-3). This test was originally developed in 1965 and is in its third version. Carrow-Woolfolk (1999) presented revised normative data to update this staple assessment tool. The TACL-3 has three subtests, each measuring specific aspects of language comprehension. The first subtest examines vocabulary comprehension; the second, grammatical morphemes, assesses the understanding of morphemes such as verb tenses, prepositions, noun number, and case. The final subtest, elaborated phrases and sentences, tests the comprehension of syntactically based word relations, and complex phrase and sentence structure. The age range for this test is 3;0 to 9;11 years.

Test of Language Competence, Expanded Edition (TLC-EE). Wiig and Secord (1989) examine metalinguistic competence with regard to semantics, syntax, and pragmatics in children, adolescents, and young adults (5;0 to 18;11). The subtests for children 5;0 to 9;11 include ambiguous sentences, making inferences, recreating speech acts, and figurative language. The level 2 subtests (9;0–18;11) cover ambiguous sentences, making inferences, recreating sentences, and figurative language. Level 2 also includes a supplemental subtest, remembering word pairs, so as to evaluate memory strategy acquisition.

Test of Problem Solving—Elementary, 3 (TOPS-3). Zachman, Huisingh, Barrett, Orman, and LoGiudice (2005) presented the third version of the TOPS, first introduced in 1984. This test integrates semantic and linguistic knowledge with reasoning ability. The test includes six subtests evaluating the child's ability to make inferences, predict outcomes, answer negative questions, sequence events, determine causes, and solve specific problems. The age range covered by the test is 6;0 to 12;11 years.

Test of Problem Solving—Adolescent (TOPS-A). Zachman, Barrett, Huisingh, Orman, and Blagden released the TOPS-A in 1991, and the revised version will be released in early 2007. The TOPS-A addresses critical thinking based on the student's language strategies using logic and experience. It focuses on a broad range of critical thinking skills. Students are presented with passages about contemporary issues and asked open-ended questions to assess clarifying, analyzing, generating solutions, evaluating, and affective thinking. The relationship between language and critical thinking requires an evaluation tool to examine an adolescent's overall approach to dealing with a situation or problem in order to see the interaction between processes rather than segment these processes into discrete skills, which would suggest they function independently of one another. The age range for this test includes 12;0 to 17;11.

❖ Informal Assessment ❖

A vital part of any communication evaluation must be a functional communication assessment or what Lahey (1988) referred to as a communication-referenced assessment. The purpose of a functional communication assessment is to determine the child's current level of functional communication and to allow for intervention planning that will build upon existing skills. Several formats have been developed to address this type of assessment (Falco, Janzen, Arick, Wilgus, & DeBoer, 1990; Janzen, 2003: Lahey, 1988). In most functional communication assessments, the format is one of observation and interview. Once this data is collected, the clinician can determine what communication skills are in place and which skills are needed most to reduce stress, anxiety, frustration, and aberrant behavior. The evaluator observes the child and may interview caregivers to determine when and how the child communicates everyday wants and needs.

The Content-Form-Use (CFU) Chart (Lahey, 1988; Adams, Bartow, & Smith, 1995) has been used to track normal language development for the past 18 years. Speech-language pathologists, who recognize the need to use the developmental model to guide treatment planning for children with autism and other communication disorders, use this chart to keep data with regard to the acquisition of semantic categories and syntactic complexity as well as the communicative function of each of the child's language productions.

Finally, portfolio assessments are becoming increasingly popular for children with autism and some with Asperger syndrome. Rather than rely on standardized test tools, one can collect representative work over a period of time to demonstrate a child's actual skills and abilities. This approach requires student and teacher participation in the selection of the pieces to be included in the portfolio (Carlson, Hagiwara, & Quinn, 1998; Duffy, Jones, & Thomas, 1999; Hendrick-Keefe, 1995; Swicegood, 1994). The portfolio should contain a table of contents or directory, an explanation of what is included and why, academic/daily living skill data, behavior/adaptive data, and more. It is important that work from every class or subject be included in the portfolio.

Who Can Diagnose Autism and Asperger Syndrome?

This question used to be much easier to answer when both autism and Asperger syndrome were viewed from a strict medical perspective. Granted, both have associated and distinct medical diagnostic criteria; however, the impact of autism and Asperger syndrome reach far beyond the confines of medical diagnoses. Autism and Asperger syndrome both impact the child, the family, the school, the community, and more. This pervasive *impact* requires the participation of medical and nonmedical professionals alike. Following diagnosis by a developmental pediatrician, neurologist, psychiatrist, or psychologist, the child with autism or Asperger syndrome will likely have significant and long-term interaction with special education teachers, speech-language pathologists, occupational and physical therapists, and others throughout the course of the educational program and beyond. That said, the ability to diagnose both autism and Asperger syndrome perhaps need not lie solely with those who can make the medical diagnoses. Clear and concise educational diagnoses are necessary to allow for potential diagnoses from an interdisciplinary team that might not include medical personnel. The American Speech-Language-Hearing Association (ASHA) recently released a position statement that supports "the SLP who has been trained in the clinical criteria for autism spectrum disorders (ASD), as well as the use of reliable and valid diagnostic and assessment tools for individuals with ASD" (p. 6) in diagnosing ASD as an independent health care professional (American Speech-Language-Hearing Association, 2006). This recommendation was predicated on the work of Filipek et al. (1999), which stated, "Language pathologists are independent health care providers who have responsibilities at the level of screening (Level1), diagnosis and evaluation (Level 2) of autism" (p. 461).

❖ Discussion Starters ❖

1. Should diagnoses be made by trained and qualified SLPs?

2. Should other professionals be able to make diagnoses if trained?

3. What are the limitations of standardized tests? The strengths?

4. What are the limitations of informal assessments? The strengths?

Chapter 5

Treatment Strategies: Looking for Evidence

Key Concepts

❖ Evidence-Based Interventions
    Pivotal Response Training
      (PRT)
    Augmentative and
      Alternative
      Communication (AAC)
    Picture Exchange
      Communication
      System (PECS)

Social Stories
Social Skill Groups
Visual Strategies
Treatment and Education
    of Autistic and
    Communication
    Handicapped Children
    (TEACCH)

In 1999, the late, great Dr. Bernard Rimland expressed a concern that many in the trenches working with children with autism also felt. R. Simpson concurred with Rimland in his 2001 article which provided an overview of applied behavior analysis (ABA). Simpson stated that the position that ABA is the "only scientifically validated treatment for autism" is "not only false, it is absurd." He continued noting that the "exclusive use of any program may be appropriate for some students, families, and professionals, but clearly would not be preferred intervention under every condition for all." (p. 70). This opinion was shared by others who called for a cessation of the apparent rivalry among treatment approaches and for recognition of the need to serve the individual child rather than the diagnosis (Brown & Bambara, 1999; Feinberg & Vacca, 2000). Janzen (2003) advocated for an integrated approach stating, "when a child, for any reason, is unable to learn automatically from the environment, teachers and parents must intervene and take a more active role— setting up the environment (the cues), providing assistance (the prompts), and arranging the consequences to ensure that important skills are learned" (p. 149).

Vital to any successful treatment program is the collection of data. Even the most talented clinician cannot rely on memory to determine the effectiveness of the treatment strategy employed. Furthermore, the emphasis on evidenced-based practice among the professions serving persons with autism requires that we know that what we are doing is truly working and effective. And, if it is not effective, we must change the plan. In the absence of data, we make decisions based on intuitions, at best, and conjecture, at the worst. We have a small window of opportunity to impact the lives of children with autism and we cannot squander that opportunity.

❖ Treatments for Autism and ❖ Asperger Syndrome

It is essential that all treatment providers and those seeking intervention services know how to actively evaluate a treatment approach prior to implementing it. In response to a request from the U.S. Department of Education, the Committee on Educational Interventions for Children with Autism was formed. The committee was charged with the integration of the scientific, theoretical, and policy literature while creating a framework for evaluating scientific evidence concerning educational interventions for young children with autism (ASHA, 2006). The committee evaluated treatments that were noted to have empirical research in a peer-reviewed journal, and measurable intervention outcomes. Interventions that had no supporting evidence were not reviewed, nor were those with "strong refuting evidence including facilitated communication and auditory integration training" (p. 16).

The committee noted three conclusions regarding their review of intervention approaches. First, the committee noted that there is empirical support for a variety of approaches addressing communication skills. Second, the committee determined that there is not sufficient research available to predict which approaches might work best for persons with autism. The committee further noted that there is no single approach that was equally effective for all persons with autism. The conclusion of the committee with regard to this issue was to recommend systematic measurement of an individual's progress using an approach, essentially suggesting a single-subject research design. The final conclusion of the committee was that more meaningful outcome measurements were needed to evaluate treatment approaches. To date, most treatment outcomes have been measured with a combination of IQ and post-intervention placement. The committee determined that these measures may not be valid as they do not measure changes in the natural learning environment. The committee encouraged the use of outcome measurements that included gains in the initiation of spontaneous communication, and generalization of these gains to environments outside the treatment context (NRC, 2001).

Effective treatment programs include early implementation, intensive instruction, inclusion of the family, ongoing assessment and program evaluation, and instruction that includes functional, spontaneous communication, social instruction in various settings, play skills with peers, skill acquisition and maintenance in natural contexts, functional assessment and positive behavioral support, and functional academic skills when determined to be appropriate (NRC, 2001).

Beckman (2002), in a review of the strategy-based approach to intervention planning, described a strategy as a plan or tool for accomplishing a task. There are four types of strategies that make up the strategy-based approach, including cognitive strategies, cuing strategies, learning strategies, and metacognitive strategies. Cognitive strategies are used to address academic tasks or social skills and include chunking, visualization, underlining, scanning, questioning, and self-checking. Cuing refers to either a visual or verbal prompt that serves as a reminder to the person to attend to learn or to use what is already learned. A learning strategy includes the steps needed to complete a specific task such as writing a story or taking a test. Metacognitive strategies (thinking about how we think) refer to how well the child with autism can understand his own learning. This means rehearsing one's learning strategy until it is stored and then accessing that learning strategy when cued and evaluating one's success at implementing the learning strategy. This is also part of self-evaluation, which is central to self-regulation.

❖ Pivotal Response Training (PRT) ❖

PRT is a service delivery model that combines a developmental approach and applied behavior analysis (ABA) procedures. PRT provides opportunities for language learning within the natural environment of the child. The approach is child centered rather than clinician centered, meaning that the child is allowed to make choices about what is to be learned, and how it is to be learned. The PRT model emphasizes the parents as primary intervention agents, but includes siblings, teachers, peers, and others who interact with the child.

Pivotal areas to be targeted in the intervention process include motivation, joint attention, responsivity to multiple cues, self-management, self-initiations, and empathy. Motivation refers to finding items or events in which the child demonstrates an interest, enough interest that the child will seek to acquire the item or initiate the event using verbal or oral communication. For example, the child may enjoy trains and may be motivated to ask for a train rather than another item. Joint attention is vital for the development of almost all skills. Joint attention requires that the child attend to the same item or event as the communication partner. Again, using the train, the child is more likely to attend to a desired item than one of less interest (Mundy, 1995). Being prepared to respond to multiple cues is required for successful navigation of nearly every environment. Studies have demonstrated that children with autism have the potential for stimulus over selectivity, or the tendency to respond to an irrelevant component of the stimulus (Koegel & Koegel, 2006; Lovaas, Schreibman, Koegel, & Rehm, 1971). Since treatment is delivered in natural environment and includes multiple agents, number of hours of intervention is very high (Koegel & Koegel, 2006). Additionally, PRT was determined to have significant evidentiary support as an effective treatment for autism (Simpson, 2005). When compared with traditional drill-based approaches, PRT has been shown to result in a higher rate of correct responding, more spontaneous utterances, and generalized language outside clinical setting, whereas drill work was noted to result in cue dependence, rote responding, lack of generalization, and increased disruptive behaviors (Koegel & Koegel, 2006). As Janzen (2003) noted the use of verbal reinforcement, "good talking" distracts the child from the powerful reinforcing outcomes of their actions. In other words, getting what you ask for is the most powerful reinforcement for using oral language. Furthermore, little disruptive behavior is observed.

PRT is useful in the classroom as this is a natural setting for children with autism. By using valid instructional strategies and embedding reinforcement in the daily program, the child with autism can practice functional skills in the environment where he or she needs to use them. PRT also provides support during the completion of homework. Allowing the child to choose the location for the work and the order the work is completed may facilitate cooperation. Using natural reinforcement such as practicing spelling with the names of favorite cartoon characters may result in greater enthusiasm and participation. The use of PRT may be limited if the personnel utilizing the technique are not adequately trained in the implementation. Inconsistent application of PRT may result in less than positive results. According to Simpson (2005), PRT is a scientifically-based practice.

❖ Augmentative and Alternative ❖ Communication (AAC)

Both aided and unaided AAC approaches have been used successfully with children with autism. Aided approaches include pictures, written cue, and speech generating devices. Unaided approaches include gestures and sign language. A meta-analysis of studies which have examined the efficacy of AAC has found most interventions to be effective with regard to behavioral change and generalization of learning (Schlosser & Lee, 2000). However, no studies can predict what system will work for individuals with autism. In fact, no data exists that support using any one system over another as systems must be designed for the individual. There is no one-size-fits-all system in this regard (NRC, 2001).

Various types of AAC approaches have been used with persons with autism and have been found to be associated with improved behavior and receptive and expressive language (Brady, 2000; Frea, Arnold, & Vittimberga, 2001; Mirenda, 2003; Schlosser, 2003). Parents often express concern that the use of AAC will inhibit the development of oral language; however, no evidence is available to support this concern (Mirenda, 2001; 2003; NRC, 2001). Since AAC has been shown to have a positive effect on behavior, it is a vital part of any comprehensive program for the child with autism who is not using oral language to get needs met. Both aided and unaided systems have been shown to be effective (Wendt, Schlosser, & Lloyd, 2004). Because AAC systems rely on visual representations, they are noted to capitalize on learning strengths in the person with autism. As AAC has also been shown to facilitate oral language and speech development rather than inhibit it, AAC approaches are also essential to any intervention program for the child with autism (Schlosser, 2003). Pairing AAC with intervention that focuses on speech-language development can be expected to improve oral output in many persons with autism. The visual support that AAC provides has been shown to improve the comprehension of language and facilitate receptive language development (NRC, 2001). See Figure 5–1 for an example of a child using an AAC device.

❖ Picture Exchange Communication ❖ System (PECS)

PECS was developed by Bondy and Frost (1994) to be utilized as an early communication modality for young children with autism. The system uses pictures (photographs or line drawings) to represent a desired item or event. These pictures are retrieved by the child and given to a communication partner who can provide the desired

Figure 5–1. A child using an AAC device.

item/event. The child does not need to demonstrate any prerequisite skills in order to begin using the PECS. The premise is that, by training the child to request highly desired items/events, the system provides immediate and functional reinforcement. In other words, the child is reinforced by getting what he or she asked for. PECS allows the child to select a communication partner by taking the picture to another person and also allows the child to initiate communicative exchanges. Simpson (2005) noted that PECS demonstrates a promising level of supportive evidence.

PECS has six phases of training and requires two adults in the initial phase of instruction. In the first phase, the child is taught, often with physical manipulation, to give a picture to another person and receives the item in return. Because hand-over-hand manipulation may be required, two adults are needed as it would be pragmatically inappropriate for the person waiting to receive the picture to also manipulate the child's exchange. Once the child has mastered the physical exchange, the second adult may not be needed.

With each phase, the task becomes more complex and at phase three, discrimination between two or more pictures is addressed. It has been noted that this phase generally takes longer than the others and can last for weeks or months. (Janzen, 2003).

Our experience has been that it is beneficial to engage in discrimination tasks early on in the process of training the child to use PECS. As a result, we use a blank card as a foil from the onset of training rather than waiting to train the child on a single picture to 80% competence. Finally, we find it essential to have the printed word accompanying every photo or line drawing so as to facilitate literacy skills from the onset. See Figure 5–2 for an example of a picture-based system.

Figure 5–2. Example of a picture-based system of communication.

❖ Social Stories ❖

Social stories serve as scripts that provide the learner with information for appropriate behaviors and social skills. According to Barry and Burlew (2004), social stories utilize empirically supported components including repetition, priming, practice, and feedback. Social stories have been found to aid in decreasing inappropriate behaviors (Adams, Gouvousis, VanLue, & Waldron, 2004; Kuoch & Mirenda, 2003; Kuttler, Miles, & Carson, 1999), while increasing positive social skills (Adams et al., 2004; Barry & Burlew, 2004; Ivey, Heflin, & Alberto, 2004).

Social stories are descriptions of social situations, including relevant social cues, and appropriate responses. A social story is effective because it presents information visually, identifies relevant social cues and describes accurate information, describes expected behavior, and lessens social interference. The need of the student provides the topic of the story. The perspective of the student provides the focus of the story. Social stories are useful because what we see as misbehavior may result from confusion. Often we assume the child with autism knows what behavior we expect, and we are frequently wrong when we make these assumptions. By reading the story immediately prior to the situation, one can provide the child with the script for the situation and facilitate success. According to Simpson (2005), social stories have shown a promising degree of evidentiary support.

Social stories can be written by anyone who can observe a problem situation. This includes parents, extended family, teachers, and other professionals. Sometimes children with autism can participate in writing their own stories. In order to write a social story, one must target a behavior or situation that is difficult for the student. Spend time looking at the situation, and practice describing the situation from the student's perspective. The story writer must consider the child's motivations, fears, current response to the situation, and the observations of others. Often it is advantageous for more than one person to observe and consider the situation as subtle nuances may be overlooked.

Social stories consist of descriptive sentences—*The teacher says when it is time for lunch. The children line up at the classroom door*; directive sentences—*I am sitting at my desk. The teacher says, "Line up for lunch." I get my lunch bag from my desk and get in line;* perspective sentences—*The teacher is happy when all the children line up for lunch. The teacher likes it when I line up with my lunch bag;* and control sentences—*I get my lunch bag and line up when my teacher tells me. When the teacher says to line up it is time for lunch.*

When crafting a social story, it is important to keep several rules in mind. While one can put one to three sentences on a page, only one concept should be addressed per page. The use of pictures or photographs may be helpful, but some children respond very concretely and fail to generalize the story beyond that represented in the illustrations. For example, a mother wrote an excellent story addressing the tying of shoes, complete with photographs of the shoe from the child's perspective. The story failed to generalize in that the child only tied the shoes depicted in the story. The writer is encouraged to avoid negative statements such as *I will not run in line to lunch,* but rather use *I will try to walk in line to lunch.*

Topics for social stories are determined by noting challenging social situations or specific social skills which need attention. Using materials that illustrate social events, present these events to the child and record misunderstandings the child might have regarding the event. For example, a comic strip that shows a boy telling a joke with his friends laughing at the punch line can be presented. Ask the child with autism or Asperger syndrome why the friends are laughing. The child might not know why they are laughing or might believe they are laughing at the boy, not the joke. This is a possible social story topic. Using this type of informal assessment can result in a number of useful topics for social stories.

As stories are generated, copies should be made and placed in notebooks. Stories that are useful at home can also be read any time at school, and those for school issues can and should be read in the home in addition to the school. It is essential however that a story for a specific event be read immediately before the event. In other words, the story for the playground must be read right before the class goes to the playground.

❖ Social Skill Groups ❖

Group intervention for children with autism and especially Asperger syndrome has been advocated by many professionals (Adams, 2005; Attwood, 1998; Marriage, Gordon, & Brand, 1995; Orzonoff & Miller,

1995). Group intervention provides opportunities for the practice of skills in a natural setting. Groups often meet at lunch in schools to allow for the practice of conversational turn taking, listening, and topic maintenance skills. Adams (2005) advocated for a specific format for group sessions that included conversation, group problem solving, and group game playing. It was noted that these three activities resulted in the greatest improvements in social behavior for children with Asperger syndrome and high functioning autism. She emphasized the importance of group problem solving as a part of every session as this type of group activity can be particularly problematic for children with Asperger syndrome and high functioning autism, in that these children tend to want to solve problems on their own, often dominating their peers. In the classroom, teachers reported that group problem solving was a frequently used teaching/learning activity and one that challenges children with Asperger syndrome and high functioning autism.

Nearly any activity can be adapted to be a group problem solving experience. For example, many children with Asperger syndrome or high functioning autism enjoy building with interlocking blocks or magnetized building materials. Build a model, take a picture of the model, and then dismantle it. Dole out the pieces to each child in the group so that no one child can complete the project alone. Present the photo of the model and explain that the group needs to figure out how to replicate the figure. Prompt the children to prompt each other so that the model can be recreated. Encourage team work and praise collaboration.

Learning to lose gracefully is essential for children with Asperger syndrome and high functioning autism. Playing games is a typical childhood activity and one from which children with Asperger syndrome and high functioning autism are often excluded. One reason for the exclusion may be their intolerance for perceived failure and their excessively negative reaction to losing. By playing simple card and board games and encouraging that the fun is in the playing not the winning, many children can learn to lose with poise, or at least without a meltdown. Randy joined the social skills program in our center when he was 7 years of age, right after receiving a diagnosis of Asperger syndrome. He could not participate in games as he would throw items or crawl under the table at the first hint that he might not win. We established our motto for games with him: "Sometimes you win, sometimes you lose. It is fun to play the game." We repeated this frequently during every game. If he had a meltdown, we continued to play and model good game manners. After about 2 months, he was able to repeat the motto, granted it was through gritted teeth and with tightly fisted hands, but he made it through the games. Now he accepts losses with ease. When he was scheduled for summer treatment and was told the wrong day to come, he told the supervisor, "It's okay, everyone makes mistakes."

Another important activity for group intervention is "what if" scenarios. It is vital that children with Asperger syndrome and high functioning autism learn to deal with real life situations and that they practice solutions to problems they may encounter in their world. For example, children with Asperger syndrome are often desperate for friends and therefore can be easily taken advantage of by others. Ned, a 9-year-old boy with Asperger syndrome, came home from school very excited because he had a new friend. His mother was excited for him and asked him what he and his friend did together. Ned reported that he carried all his friend's books for him all day long. Ned's mother was very disheartened and asked that we discuss friends and how they should treat each other in our group sessions. We created a number of "what if" scenarios and talked at length about how friends should treat each other and what is not acceptable. While role-play can be helpful for some with Asperger syndrome, it is not always an effective strategy as the child with Asperger syndrome may consider it pretending and not recognize its value as practice for a real world situation. For more information and ideas for group intervention activities, see Adams (2005).

❖ Visual Strategies: Types and Descriptions ❖

There are various types of visual support strategies available for use with children on the spectrum. Generally, there is evidence to support the use of these techniques with children with autism and Asperger syndrome (Janzen, 2003). The following are commonly used, but not all have been subjected to evaluation for efficiency and efficacy.

- ❖ Visual schedules—daily and mini
- ❖ Checklists
- ❖ Cue cards
- ❖ Color-coded materials

Visual Schedules. Nearly all of us use visual schedules in some form or another, but we do not always consider their use with young children. For the young child who is not yet reading, a picture-based schedule can be used to detail the day's events. Furthermore, mini-picture schedules can be developed to assist the child in the independent completion of tasks. For example, a mini-schedule could be placed in the bathroom detailing the steps to successful daily hygiene (*Wash your face. Brush your teeth. Brush your hair*). For some children, a mini- or embedded schedule can be created to illustrate the steps to brushing the teeth. Visual schedules are always oriented in a top-down fashion so that they can be differentiated from communication systems that are oriented from left to right. See Figure 5–3 for a simple visual schedule.

Generally, the sooner schedules can be implemented in the daily life of the child, the better. The schedule can serve to diminish problems with transitions from one activity to the next, and can reduce anxiety and fears with regard to what is coming next. Ultimately, visual schedules can foster independence as the child learns to move throughout the day with little or no need for adult intervention. The schedule can and should grow with the child. For the young child an object- or picture-based schedule can be used, always with accompanying print. As the child develops skills, the schedule may transition to a print-only format. This can take the form of a laminated schedule placed on a desk/work space, or a daily planner. Some older children will demonstrate skills to utilize electronic devices such as a personal digital assistant (PDA) (Ferguson, Myles, & Hagiwara, 2005). As technology develops by leaps and bounds, cell phones now include calendar functions as well as phone and address books, to allow for successful personal organization and self-management.

Checklists. Certainly, we have all made a list of things that we have to do. Perhaps our lists name chores or tasks that we hope to accomplish over a week's time. For the child with autism or Asperger syndrome, the list might be for things that the child needs to accomplish in the next hour. If the child is in study hall, the checklist may include the list of assignments facing the child. The child may complete the items and check them off the list. Later, the list may be referenced again at home to ensure that all assignments are completed prior to the next school day.

For maximum flexibility, dry erase boards are available in all shapes and sizes. Many boards come with magnets allowing them

Figure 5-3.
Example of a
simple visual
schedule.

to be placed on home appliances or inside a school locker. Items can be checked or marked off the list and the boards can be easily erased and a new list created as needed. The markers for such boards also come in a variety of colors allowing color coding of tasks to facilitate organization. School related tasks might be written in red, while play or sports related tasks could be written in blue. This makes the list easily scanned by adults and helps children learn to categorize similar tasks or events.

To facilitate participation in daily living activities, checklists allow the child to help with shopping or other errands. For example, the child can be given a portion of the grocery list for which she is responsible. She checks off the items as they are purchased, making her essential to successful shopping. This can also occupy the child's attention, reducing distractions that might cause aberrant behavior. When the family has a number of errands to run, it is important that the child be kept involved and busy. Giving the child a card with the names of all the stores to be visited allows her to remain focused and helps her know when the errands will be completed.

Cue Cards. When the child with autism/Asperger syndrome is faced with delivering a verbal message, the stress of the situation may impact the child's ability to transmit that message. A cue card allows the child to relay a message by referencing the card. The child can use the card as a cue to assist in transmitting the verbal message, or if that proves too challenging the child can simply pass the card to the communication partner (Janzen, 2003). Cue cards can be printed for a variety of situations, color coded for topics, laminated, hole punched, and then placed on a C ring. The ring allows for the easy addition or removal of cards. It also allows the cards to be clipped to the child's belt loop or book bag. Cue cards can be expanded to include a short list of options for addressing a social situation, like how to enter a conversation. The key to using the cue card is not to overwhelm the user with excessive information or language. Keep it clear and concise. See Figure 5–4 for cue cards on a C ring, which allows for portability.

A situation that might lend itself to cue cards is greeting a new person. The cue card contains the language needed for the greeting and helps the child know that he has been successful in the exchange. It also lets him know when the exchange is completed.

Color-Coded Materials. To address executive function issues, color-coded materials may prove helpful. Families and teachers are

Figure 5–4. Cue cards on a "c" ring for easy access.

encouraged to utilize systems using color to help the child with autism develop and maintain self-management skills. Using colored file folders and closable colored plastic sleeves, the child's school work can be organized by subject. Placing the file folder for assignment pages, worksheets, homework, a notebook, and pencils/pens in the plastic sleeve, along with texts and workbooks, creates a manageable packet the child can retrieve for each class or subject.

This is particularly helpful when children with autism enter the later elementary grades and middle and high school where they have to change classes and have more materials to keep up with. By placing a legend on the child's desk or inside the locker, the child can match the appropriate packet for the next class. At the end of the day, the child can place the packets needed for homework or other class work in the book bag to take home.

For the home, color coding on a monthly calendar can help the child with autism know which days are school days and which are not. Using colored adhesive disks, the parents and child can place one color on school days and another color on weekends and holidays. This can be particularly helpful as teacher workdays can disrupt a child's rhythm. Most schools announce workdays and holidays well in advance allowing for this type of planning. Additional colors can be added for sports, therapies, and other daily/weekly events. Color coding allows children with autism and Asperger syndrome to develop self-management skills, learning to prepare themselves for the day's events by recognizing the colors. For example, colored file folders can be used for organizing a child's work.

❖ Treatment and Education of Autistic ❖ and Communication Handicapped Children (TEACCH)

The TEACCH model for intervention was developed in North Carolina and is the brainchild of Eric Scholper; it is used with great success around the world. Randall and Parker (1999) chose the TEACCH model as a desirable model over others because of the following characteristics: respect for the person with autism, respect for the parents and families of the person with autism, inclusion of the caregivers in all aspects of treatment planning and service delivery, in-depth knowledge of autism as it impacts all aspects of child development by professional personnel, open-mindedness of personnel, long-term data to support the approach, a comprehensive program serving the person with autism into adulthood, and adaptability of the approach as evidenced by its adoption in non-English speaking countries.

TEACCH is not a technique or even a collection of techniques. It is a model for comprehensive treatment delivery that allows for the development of treatment plans based on an individual's specific needs, as opposed to a one-size-fits-all checklists. TEACCH lists as its main objective the improvement in communication skills and autonomy so that the person with autism can reach her maximum potential. Rather than focusing on behaviors, as most behavior modification programs do, the TEACCH model serves to address the underlying causes of the aberrant behaviors, thereby increasing adaptation and lessening behavior difficulties. The result of this approach is that the person with autism can begin to better communicate wants and needs and recognize that she can impact the behavior of others effectively to get needs met. Additionally, by beginning with a simple atmosphere of success, we can gradually increase the complexity of the tasks and the environment, and we can increase autonomy.

For example, a young child was a full-time participant in a kindergarten classroom with one-on-one assistance available at all times. He had a work station in the classroom with an in box, a work space, and an out box. He also had his PECS book and visual schedule available at his station. He practiced discrete trial activities at this space with upcoming work placed in the in box and work moved from left to right into the out box. The classroom curriculum was adapted by his mother and teacher. When he was able to effectively join the group for activities, he did so. When he needed a sensory break, he asked for one with his PECS book. This is an excellent illustration of the integrated TEACCH approach. See Table 5–1 for a summary of the treatments discussed.

Table 5–1. Intervention Strategies and Evidence/Empirical Support

Intervention Strategy	Level of Evidence/ Empirical Support
Pivotal Response Training (PRT)	Scientifically-based practice
Augmentative Alternative Communication (AAC)	Promising practice
Picture Exchange Communication System (PECS)	Promising practice
Social Stories	Promising practice
Social Skill Groups	Promising practice
Visual Schedules	Anecdotal support
Checklists	Anecdotal support
Cue Cards	Anecdotal support
Color-Coded Materials	Anecdotal support
Treatment and Education of Autistic and Communication Handicapped Children (TEACCH)	Promising support

Adapted from "Evidence-Based Practices and Students with Autism Spectrum Disorders," by R. Simpson, 2005, *Focus on Autism and Other Developmental Disabilities, 20*, pp. 140–149. Reprinted with permission

❖ Discussion Starters ❖

1. What are the strengths and limitations of each treatment approach presented?

2. Brainstorm an integrated treatment approach for a person with autism and for a person with Asperger syndrome.

3. Write a social story for a problem a child with autism might encounter.

4. Brainstorm activities for social skill group intervention.

Chapter 6

Challenging Behaviors: Facing the Meltdown

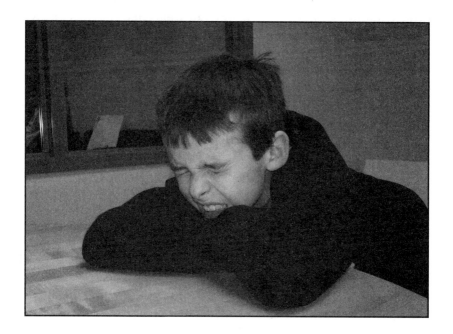

Key Concepts

❖ Behavior Challenges

❖ Functional Analysis of Behavior
  Functional Equivalence
  Form of Behavior

❖ Positive Behavioral Support

❖ Contracts

❖ Behavior Reduction

❖ Intervention for Behavior Challenges ❖

Temper tantrum . . . cruddy behavior . . . screaming, ugly fit . . . meltdown. Call it what you will, the challenging behavior we will call the *meltdown* is a source of frustration and concern for most parents of children with autism and Asperger syndrome. When faced with a difficult task, a transition, or the word *no*, the child may protest intensely, physically, and loudly. Parents may find this behavior outburst to be manageable in some situations, while embarrassing and unsettling in others.

Perhaps the most important thing to be understood with regard to the meltdown is that the parent, teacher, caregiver, whomever, cannot allow him- or herself to be controlled by the threat of the meltdown. The adult cannot be afraid of the meltdown. If the child begins to believe that the meltdown is a means to an end, than the behavior outburst has become a form of manipulation. We ask parents what they would do if their non-autistic child threw a temper tantrum in the local department store. Most state without hesitation that they would immediately remove the child from the store. However, the same parents will buy their child with autism a toy that has been demanded just to avoid a scene. This disparity is not lost in the nonaffected child, and can result in problem behavior in that child. What should the caregiver do when faced with a meltdown? The adult is encouraged to ignore the meltdown, not the child. Calmly (fake it if you must) remove the child from the situation. Do not try to explain or calm with words, as words can serve to confuse a calm child and are likely lost in the child when in the throes of a meltdown. Ultimately, the caregivers must determine what function the meltdown serves and replace it with a functional behavior.

Wing (1996) noted six rules that parents need to consider when dealing with their child. First and foremost, parents must understand reinforcement and the value of rewards. Parents need help in determining a list of reinforcers or a reinforcement menu from which the parent can choose a reward for positive behavior. Secondly, parents need to understand the value of manipulating the antecedent, or what comes before the problem behavior. For example, a child in a preschool classroom screamed whenever there was a fire drill. This drill was the antecedent. In some cases, the problem behavior can be averted just by changing or removing the antecedent. While fire drills could not be stopped, the child was warned ahead of time and screams were avoided. Thirdly, Wing notes the importance of including extended family in training for behavior management. All caregivers/adults must adhere to the same behavior plan. If one person accepts a problem behavior, the child can become confused when another person does not accept the same problem behavior. The fourth principle is that it is better to replace a problem behavior with an adaptive or functional skill rather than constantly punishing the challenging behavior in hopes of extinguishing it. The problem behavior may disappear if the child has an effective replacement behavior. Next, it is essential that the response to a challenging or acceptable behavior be immediate. Both reinforcement and punishment must be administered contingent upon the target behavior. Finally, parents need to understand that behavior change takes time and consistency. Parents must recognize that strategies take time to be effective and that changing strategies after a brief trial period does not contribute to success. If a strategy is not working, the caregiver must ensure that the strategy is being properly implemented by all adults involved. The adults should not assume that the strategy is failing until they have tried it for an extended period of time with insurance that all caregivers are using the strategy in the same way.

❖ Functional Analysis of Behavior ❖

Functional analysis of behavior is an effective measure for addressing behaviors of concern through four steps. By observing a situation, developing a hypothesis regarding the function of the behavior, and implementing an intervention strategy, we can reduce problem behaviors. Step one involves determining a target behavior and observing and measuring that target behavior. For example, the child with autism may have a problem hitting people. It is important to determine who is being hit, and in response to what. This not the time to focus on why the behavior is occurring.

The second step requires that the observer note the behavior, its antecedents, and the consequences following the behavior. This is commonly referred to as the ABC approach. The response of the child to the consequences is also an important part of this analysis. It is important to note what immediately precedes the targeted behavior as that can be manipulated. This will be discussed further in the section regarding positive behavioral support. Using the example of the child who is hitting, the observer notes when the hitting occurs, what happened right before the hitting, and the consequence of the hitting. It is probably easiest to construct a simple three-column form with the headings antecedent, behavior, and consequence. The observer merely makes the observations and does not attempt to address the "why."

Step three addresses hypothesis formation. It is during this step that the observer formulates a hypothesis or theory as to why the targeted behavior occurs, what the function of the behavior is, and what purpose the behavior serves. Again utilizing our example of hitting, the observation revealed that the child hit every time he had to transition from free time/play to activities completed at the seat or desk. The observation data revealed that he did not refuse to complete the seat/desk work, and that he did not hit during these activities.

The final step allows for testing of the hypothesis. During this phase, the antecedents and consequences are manipulated to determine the validity of the hypothesis. Taking our example, we can manipulate antecedents to test the theory that the child is hitting as a result of the need to transition, not because of the requirement to complete seat/desk work. By trying different antecedents, we can determine if our theory is correct and how best to deal with the problem behavior. One manipulation included showing the child what was going to take place at the seat/desk. On days when the group was going to color, he was shown the picture to be colored and his crayons. When a book was being read, he was shown the book. He was able to see what was coming next, and why it was important for him to leave free time/play. Once a visual schedule was implemented that showed what would happen after free time, the child was able to make the transition without hitting. Table 6–1 illustrates a simple ABC chart.

❖ Positive Behavioral Support ❖

Behaviors are messages!
That is the foundation of positive behavioral support (PBS). The fundamental principle is that behaviors have communicative value. Whether these behaviors are positive or negative, they can commu-

Table 6–1. Sample of Simple ABC Chart for Functional Analysis of Behavior

Antecedent	Behavior	Consequence
Teacher announced transition to lunch	Beth yelled "No" and stayed at her desk working on her math paper	Class late to lunch; teacher asked Beth to join class; Beth did after work done
Teacher told Beth to finish her reading work sheet	Beth tore up the paper	Beth was given a time out
Bell rang for fire drill	Beth plugged her ears, crawled under the desk	Beth coaxed out with offer of treat
Time for PE announced	Beth ran out of the room to gym	None observed
Science lesson presented	Beth hummed loudly	Removed from room for 10 minutes until lesson over
Child bumped into Beth's chair	Beth hit her and said "Get away"	Beth given time out

nicate wants and needs, frustrations and excitement. We can use the principles of PBS to increase the child's skills and adaptability to thereby decrease problem behaviors. We can replace the problem behavior with more functional, socially acceptable behaviors that get the same desired result.

PBS is different from traditional behavior modification. While the focus of traditional behavior modification is to decrease problem behavior, the focus of PBS is to increase skills and adaptations. Rather than spending time trying to get rid of a problem behavior by punishment, PBS attempts to decrease the problem behavior by replacing it with a functional skill. By increasing adaptations, the child has more skills to call upon in different situations, and should have to rely less on problem behaviors for communication.

Traditional behavior modification focuses on the form of the behavior, and PBS focuses on the function of the behavior. What this means is that what the behavior looks like is not as important as what the behavior means or what purpose it serves. What has been noted is that one behavior may have many functions and one function can take many forms. This is an illustration of the principle of functional equivalence. This means that a child may hit, scream, and cry to communicate fear or the child may hit to communicate fear, frustration, and hunger. The point is that looking at the form of the behavior will not help you decrease the behavior. You must attempt to determine what function or purpose the behavior serves. Once this has been determined, one can try and replace the problem behavior with something recognizable for its communicative intent. This may be the sign for *eat* replacing the hitting. This can include the child giving a picture representing the need for a break when frustration rises in response to classroom demands. This may mean using the word *stop* when the child is frightened.

Traditional behavior modification emphasizes consequence manipulation, while PBS recognizes that attention needs to be focused on the antecedent, what happens right before the behavior. Behavior modification that focuses on consequences only misses what might trigger the problem behavior. Those who live and work with children with autism and Asperger syndrome report that the use of time out has little impact on problem behavior. In fact, many note that time out seems to be a positive experience for some children with autism and Asperger syndrome. Consider the child who is tearing up his papers to avoid completing his work. Removing him from the classroom to a time out space essentially reinforces the paper tearing behavior. It says to the child, "If you want to get out of work *and* the classroom where demands are made, tear up your papers."

Functional analysis of behavior is a vital component of PBS. It is what allows the teacher or caregiver to develop theories about behaviors, test them, and intervene. The steps of functional analysis were discussed in the previous section. Once the analysis has been completed, PBS dictates that we intervene beginning with alterations. We do not seek to alter the person first; rather, we examine the environment and determine if an adjustment there can alleviate the problem behavior without disenfranchising others or unduly taxing the caregiver or teacher.

For example, there was a child, Frank, in a preschool program who was screaming, kicking, and hitting for "no apparent reason." Following a functional analysis, it was determined that Frank was reacting every time a door opened in the classroom. There were two doors into the room, one leading to the hallway with the restroom and one opening onto the main hall of the school. The hallway door was opened frequently by other faculty wanting to visit the preschool class and see the adorable preschoolers. The door to the restroom was usually but not only used for the restroom. A rule was established that the restroom door was used only for the restroom and that the hall door was used only when necessary. Restricting the use of the restroom door to restroom trips only made that door's opening and closing more predictable. Frank did not need to be concerned with that door. Once the use of the main door was limited, Frank still reacted, but since the door opened much less often, he had fewer outbursts. Additionally, the staff now knew that his behavior was related to the door and could predict his behavior with greater accuracy. You will note that no time was spent initially trying to understand why Frank had the outbursts, nor was attention focused on the different types of aberrant behaviors Frank demonstrated. But why did Frank react so negatively to the door opening? We find from persons with high functioning autism that doors are a particular source of anxiety as their opening signals change is about to occur, someone will enter or leave, thereby changing the dynamics of the situation.

If attempts to alter the environment do not yield the desired change in behavior, alteration of the curriculum is the next step. Adapting the curriculum to facilitate success may reduce problem behaviors. A child with autism, Henry, was fully included in a kindergarten class but was not yet able to form letters to write his name. One of his objectives was that he be able to recognize and write his name. Rather than focus on the paper and pencil aspect of the task, the curriculum was adapted to meet his needs. He preferred upper case letters so a complete set of letters was made in the upper case. A strip of Velcro was placed in a sentence strip. Henry was then allowed to "write" his name by placing the letters for his name on the strip. He was also allowed to write his other target words this way. He responded well to this adaptation and was able to first match his name and then place the letters without a model.

Finally, if the alterations to the environment and curriculum have not resulted in the desired changes, we seek to alter the person by increasing his skills and adaptations. We do this by improving the person's communication skills. We try to improve oral language and gestural communication and use alternative communication means as needed. If the focus is on functional communication skills, we stand to have the biggest impact on aberrant behaviors. If a child does not have a conventional or at least recognizable communication means, he will use what he has available. That may be hitting, screaming, or throwing. By providing effective communication, we help the child with autism learn to navigate the challenges of his or her world.

❖ Contracts ❖

A strategy that has been found to be useful for dealing with behavior concerns is a behavioral contract. Contracts can be used to teach new skills and behaviors or to eliminate problem behaviors. Additionally, contracts can be used to maintain existing functional skills. The development of the contract requires the participation of the caregivers, teachers, extended family, and the person with autism/Asperger syndrome, and serves as an agreement among all involved as to each party's role and responsibility. The contract should clearly delineate the expected behaviors and consequences (Downing, 1990; Myles & Simpson, 2003). Jerrod, a middle school-aged boy with Asperger syndrome, was enrolled in a social skills group. He wanted to graduate from the group, but still had several problem behaviors at school. The teacher, his mother, the group clinician, and Jerrod worked together to craft the contract which, upon completion, would allow him to graduate from intervention. Items on the list included not "buzzing" the teacher (making a loud buzzer noise) when she misspoke or Jerrod disagreed with her, and not arguing with her about assignments.

❖ Behavior Reduction ❖

On occasion, it is important to target the reduction of an aberrant behavior. In that instance, the undesired behavior must be followed by either punishment or the withdrawal of reinforcement. Once it has been established that the child can demonstrate the desired positive behavior, a program can be implemented to extinguish the undesirable behavior. It should be noted that behavior reduction interventions can result in power struggles with persons who present with Asperger syndrome. Children with Asperger syndrome tend to engage in power struggles anyway and punishment or loss of privileges can cause an escalation in these struggles. Behavior reduction strategies should only be implemented after it has been determined that positive behavioral interventions have proven unsuccessful. Additionally, these behavior reduction strategies are useful when the undesired behavior has the potential to cause harm to the individual or place the individual or anyone else in danger. If such a strategy is to be used, a clear plan for its implementation must be created and strictly adhered to by all with whom the person interacts.

When choosing a consequence to eliminate or at least reduce a problem behavior, it is important to consider the following points. Choose a consequence that the child does not like. While that seems like a no-brainer, some things are more aversive to the child than others and will be more powerful as a consequence. Always remember that consequences are given out without anger. Never punish in anger as it can result in the child feeling attacked rather than punished for a bad behavior. All consequences must be administered contingent on the behavior. A delay in the consequence diminishes the power of the consequence. In fact, if too much time passes between the behavior and the consequences, the child may not realize that the two things are related. Finally, make sure that the punishment fits the crime. In other words, the consequence should be an appropriate response to the offense (Kaufman & Lord Larson, 2005). David, a sixth-grader with Asperger syndrome, was accused of writing on a bathroom wall. The consequence was that he was made to clean feces from another bathroom stall. This consequence does not seem to be related to the offense. A more logical consequence would have been to have the child remove the writing, and perhaps touch up the paint in the stall.

❖ Discussion Starters ❖

1. Observe a child with autism or Asperger syndrome and complete an ABC chart.

2. Develop a PBS plan for a child with autism or Asperger syndrome.

3. Write a contract for a child with Asperger syndrome.

Chapter 7

The Future:
Where Do We Go From Here?

Key Concepts

❖ Cause/Etiology

❖ Conclusions

❖ Research Needed

We know that autism and Asperger syndrome are neurological disorders that can result in deficits in cognitive, academic, social, and communication functioning. We know that autism and Asperger syndrome impact all ethnic, racial, and socioeconomic groups. We know that boys tend to be affected more often than girls. We know a great deal more than we did just a few short years ago.

Both autism and Asperger syndrome have shown distinct increases in prevalence rates in recent years. While this is likely due, in part, to the revised diagnostic criteria put forward in the last 15 years, it also appears that we may be seeing more children with both disorders. Certainly, more children are being diagnosed than ever before and as a result, the already limited services available are being stretched to the maximum.

There is still no consensus as to the causes of autism and Asperger syndrome although both appear to have a genetic basis, but what might flip on that genetic switch may differ greatly among persons on the spectrum. We do know that there appear to be at least two subgroups of children on the spectrum, those who seem to be born with symptoms of autism and those who seem to follow a course of normal development up until about 18 months of age when regression is noted. We have not yet determined what might cause these two courses of the disorders.

❖ Where Do We Go from Here? ❖

We need to ensure there is a continued focus on the causes of autism and Asperger syndrome. Once the causes are determined, one would hope that the disorders could be prevented. While that is a meaningful and vital goal, research must also focus on treatment efficacy. Parents of children with autism and Asperger syndrome may be among the most vulnerable of parents as there is still a great deal of mystery and confusion surrounding the disorders. With an often heightened sense of urgency, parents may be vulnerable to paying for interventions for which there is little or no evidence of effectiveness. We cannot take the attitude that we will just "try it and see" as the window of opportunity for meaningful intervention has been shown to be opened the widest in the first few years. No one wants to expend energy, time, and money on treatments that do not afford long-term, sustainable changes.

We need research that addresses efficacious intervention for reading and writing issues among those with autism and Asperger syndrome. We need research that examines teaching strategies that support mathematics and language arts instruction. We need research that supports effective behavioral interventions. We need research that supports all aspects of intervention so that we can say with some level of assuredness that what we are doing is right for each and every child we serve.

We need to ensure that education of professionals takes place in a fashion that virtually guarantees that all children with autism and Asperger syndrome are diagnosed and receiving services as soon as possible. Best practice guidelines for pediatricians advocate for routine screening for autism at well-baby checks (American Academy of Pediatrics, 2001). This is not a universal practice or we would not have children with a significant degree of autism arrive at school the first day of kindergarten with no diagnosis, and no early intervention services. We would not have children being diagnosed with Asperger syndrome only after they have been labeled with attention deficits, behavior disorders, and academic problems in spite of normal cognitive potential.

While writing this book, we note that the United States House of Representatives just approved Senate Bill 843, the Combating Autism Act, which authorizes $860,000,000 in federal funding to support autism-related research, early detection, and intervention through 2011. Hopefully, when you read this, this important legislation will have been signed into law and children and families impacted by autism and Asperger syndrome will be reaping the benefits.

❖ Discussion Starters ❖

1. What is the latest research relative to the cause of autism and Asperger syndrome?

2. What new treatments are being used to help children with autism and Asperger syndrome?

3. Do the new treatments have empirical support?

References

Achenbach, T. M., & Rescoria, L. (2001). *Child Behavior Checklist for Ages 6-18 (CBCL/6-18)*. Burlington, VT: University of Vermont, Research Center for Children, Youth, & Families.

Adams, L. (1998). Oral-motor and motor-speech characteristics of children with autism. *Focus on Autism and Other Developmental Disabilities, 13*(2), 108-113.

Adams, L. (2005). *Group treatment for Asperger syndrome: A social skill curriculum*. San Diego, CA: Plural.

Adams, L., Bartow, M., & Smith, J. (1995). *150 sequential language activities: Based on the Bloom and Lahey models*. Tucson, AZ: Communication Skill Builders.

Adams, L., Gouvousis, A., VanLue, M., & Waldron, C. (2004). Social story intervention: Improving communication skills in a child with autism spectrum disorder. *Focus on Autism and Other Developmental Disabilities, 19*(2), 87-94.

Adams, L., & Vinsh, D. (2003). *Oral motor and motor-speech characteristics in children and adolescents with autism*. Unpublished manuscript, Radford University, Radford, VA.

American Academy of Pediatrics. (2001). Technical report: The pediatrician's role in the diagnosis and management of autistic spectrum disorder. *Pediatrics, 107*, 1221-1226.

American Psychiatric Association. (2000). *Diagnostic and statistical manual of mental disorders* (4th ed., text rev.) Washington, DC: Author.

American Speech-Language-Hearing Association. (2006). *Guidelines for speech-language pathologists in diagnosis, assessment, and treatment for autism spectrum disorders across the life span*. Retrieved March 16, 2007 from http://www.asha.org/members/deskref-journal/deskref/default

Attwood, T. (1998). *Asperger's syndrome: A guide for parents and professionals*. London: Jessica Kingsley.

Bagenholm, A., & Gillberg, C. (1991). Psychosocial effects on siblings of children with autism and mental retardation: A population based study. *Journal of Mental Deficiency Research, 35*, 291-307.

Bagnato, S. J., Neisworth, J. T., Salvia, J. J., & Hunt, F. M. (1999). *Temperament and Atypical Behavior Scale (TABS): Early childhood indicators of developmental dysfunction*. Baltimore: Paul H. Brookes.

Barnhill, G., Hagiwara, T., Myles, B., Simpson, R., Brick, M., & Griswold, D. (2000). Parent, teacher and self report of problems and adaptive behaviors in children and adolescents with Asperger syndrome. *Diagnostique*, *25*, 147–167.

Baron-Cohen, S. (1990). Autism: A specific cognitive disorder of "mindblindness." *International Review of Psychiatry*, *2*, 81–90.

Baron-Cohen, S., Allen, J., & Gillberg, C. (1992). Can autism be detected at 18 months? The needle, the haystack, and the CHAT. *British Journal of Psychiatry*, *161*, 839–843.

Baron-Cohen, S., O'Riordan, M., Stone, V., Jones, R., & Palisted, K. (1999). Recognition of faux pas by normally developing children and children with Asperger syndrome or high-functioning autism. *Journal of Autism and Developmental Disorders*, *29*(5), 407–418.

Barry, L., & Burlew, S. (2004). Using social stories to teach choice and play skills to children with autism. *Focus on Autism and Other Developmental Disabilities*, *19*, 45–51.

Barthélémy, S., Roux, S., Adrien, J. L., Hameury, L., Guérin, B., Garreau, M., et al. (1997). Validation of the Revised Behavior Summarized Evaluation Scale, *Journal of Autism and Developmental Disorders*, *27*, 139–153.

Beckman, P. (2002). *Strategy instruction* (ERIC Report No. E638). Retrieved January 5, 2006, from the Council of Exceptional Children's Information Center on Disabilities and Gifted Education: http://www.ericec.org/digests/e638.html

Blankenship, K. (2000). *Theory of mind and children with learning disabilities*. Unpublished master's thesis, Radford University, Radford, VA.

Bligh, S. (2000) *Social Language Groups* [video recording]. Shawnee Mission, KS: Autism Asperger.

Bondy, A., & Frost, L. (1994). The picture exchange system. *Focus on Autistic Behavior*, *9*(3), 1–19.

Bracken, B., & McCallum, S. (2002). *Universal Nonverbal Intelligence Test*. Rolling Meadows, IL: Riverside.

Brady, N. (2000). Improved comprehension of object names following voice output communication aid use: Two case studies. *Augmentative and Alternative Communication*, *16*, 197–204.

Brown, C., & Dunn, W. (2002). *Adolescent/Adult Sensory Profile*. San Antonio, TX: Harcourt Assessment.

Brown, F., & Bambara, L. (1999). Special series on interventions for young children with autism. *Journal of the Association of Persons with Severe Handicaps*, *24*, 131–132.

Brown, L., Sherbenou, R., & Johnsen, S. (2000). *Test of Nonverbal Intelligence* (3rd ed.). Minneapolis, MN: AGS.

Bryson, S. E. (1997). Epidemiology of autism: Overview and issues outstanding. In D. J. Cohen & F. R. Volkmar (Eds.), *Handbook of autism and pervasive developmental disorders* (2nd ed., pp. 41–46). New York: John Wiley & Sons.

Carlson, J., Hagiwara, T., & Quinn, C. (1998). Assessment of students with autism. In R. L. Simpson & B. S. Myles (Eds.), *Educating children and youth with autism: Strategies for effective practice* (pp. 25–54). Austin, TX: Pro-Ed.

Carrow-Woolfolk, E. (1999) *Test for Auditory Comprehension of Language—3*. Austin, TX: Pro-Ed.

Centers for Disease Control and Prevention. (n.d.). *How common are ASDs?* Retrieved October 17, 2006, from http://www.cdc.gov/ncbddd/autism

Courchesne, E., Akshoomoff, N., Egaas, B., Lincoln, A., Saitoh, O., Schreibman, L., et al. (1994). Role of cerebellar and parietal dysfunction in the social and cognitive deficits in patients with infantile autism. In Autism Society of America (Ed.), *Autism Society of America Conference Proceedings, 1994* (pp.19–21). Arlington, TX: Future Education.

Delacato, C. (1974). *The ultimate stranger: The autistic child.* Novato, CA: Arena Press.

Downing, J. (1990). Contingency contracts: A step-by-step format. *Intervention in School and Clinic, 26,* 111–113.

Duffy, M., Jones, J., & Thomas, S. (1999). Using portfolios to foster independent thinking. *Intervention in School and Clinic, 35,* 34–37.

Dunn, W. (1999). *Sensory Profile.* San Antonio, TX: Harcourt Assessment.

Dunn, W. (2002). *Infant/Toddler Sensory Profile.* San Antonio, TX: Harcourt Assessment.

Durand, V. M., & Crimmins, D. (1992). *Motivation Assessment Scale (MAS).* Topeka, KS: Monaco and Associates.

Ehlers, S., & Gillberg, C. (1999). A screening questionnaire for Asperger syndrome and other high-functioning autism spectrum disorders in school age children. *Journal of Autism and Developmental Disorders, 29*(2), 129–141.

Falco, R., Janzen, J., Arick, J., Wilgus, K., & DeBoer, M. (1990). *Project QUEST in-service manual: Functional assessment of student needs and functional instruction for communication, social interactions, self-management, and choice.* Portland, OR: Department of Special and Counselor Education, Portland State University.

Feinberg, E., & Vacca, J. (2000). The drama and trauma of creating policies on autism: Critical issues to consider in the new millennium. *Focus on Autism and Other Developmental Disabilities, 15,* 130–137.

Ferguson, H., Myles, B., & Hagiwara, T. (2005). Using a personal digital assistant to enhance the independence of an adolescent with Asperger syndrome. *Education and Training in Developmental Disabilities, 40*, 60-67.

Filipek, P., Accardo, D., Baranek, G., Cook, E., Dawson, G., Gordon, B., et al (1999) The screening and diagnosis of autism spectrum disorders. *Journal of Autism and Developmental Disorders, 29*, 439-484.

Fisman, S., & Wolf, L. (1991). The handicapped child: Psychological effects of parental, marital and sibling relationships. *Psychiatric Clinics of North America, 14*, 199-217.

Frea, W., Arnold, C., & Vittimberga, G. (2001). A demonstration of the effects of augmentative communication on extreme aggressive behavior of a child with autism within an integrated preschool setting. *Journal of Positive Behavior Interventions, 3*, 194-198.

Frith, U. (1991). *Autism: Explaining the enigma.* Oxford, UK: Basil Blackwell, Ltd.

Frith, U. (1992). *Autism and Asperger syndrome.* Cambridge, UK: Cambridge University Press.

Fullerton, A., Stratton, J., Coyne, P., & Gray, C. (1996). *Higher functioning adolescents and young adults with autism.* Austin, TX: Pro-Ed.

Ghaziuddin, M., & Mountain-Kimchi, K. (2004). Defining the intellectual profile of Asperger syndrome: Comparison with high-functioning autism. *Journal of Autism and Developmental Disorders, 34*, 279-284.

Gillberg, C. (1990). *Diagnosis and treatment of autism.* New York: Plenum Press.

Gillberg, C., & Coleman, M. (1992). *Biology of the autistic syndromes* (2nd ed.). London: MacKeith Press.

Gilliam, J. (1995). *Gilliam Autism Rating Scale (GARS).* Austin, TX: Pro-Ed.

Gilliam, J. E. (2001). *Gilliam Asperger Disorder Scale.* Austin, TX: Pro-Ed.

Glascoe, F. (1997). *Parents' evaluation of developmental status.* Nashville, TN: Ellsworth & Vandermeer Press.

Grandin, T. (1984). My experiences as an autistic child: A review of selected literature. *Journal of Orthomolecular Psychiatry, 13*, 144-174.

Grandin, T. (1992). An inside view of autism. In E. Schopler & G. Mesibov (Eds.), *High functioning individuals with autism* (pp. 105-126). New York: Plenum.

Grandin, T., & Scariano, M. (1986). *Emergence: Labeled autistic.* Novato, CA: Arena Press.

Greenspan, S. I., DeGangi, G., & Wieder, S. (2001). *Functional Emotional Assessment Scale for Infancy and Early Childhood (FEAS).* Bethesda, MD: The Interdisciplinary Council on Developmental and Learning Disorders.

Griswold, D., Barnhill, G., Myles, B., Hagiwara, T., & Simpson, R. (2002). Asperger syndrome and academic achievement. *Focus on Autism and Other Developmental Disabilities,17*, 94–102.

Harrison, P. (1985). *Vineland Adaptive Behavior Scales (VABS)* (classroom edition). Circle Pines, MN: American Guidance Service.

Hendrick-Keefe, C. (1995). Portfolios: Mirrors of learning. *Teaching Exceptional Children, 27*, 66–67.

Howlin, P. (1988). Living with impairment: The effects on children having an autistic sibling. *Child: Care, Health and Development, 14*, 395–408.

Ivey, M., Heflin, J., & Alberto, P. (2004). The use of social stories to promote independent behaviors in novel events for children with PDD-NOS. *Focus on Autism and Other Developmental Disabilities, 19*, 164–176.

Janzen, J. (2003). *Understanding the nature of autism: A practical guide.* San Antonio, TX: Psychological Corporation.

Johnston, J. (1982). Narratives: A new look at communication problems in older language-disordered children. *Language, Speech, and Hearing Services in Schools, 13*, 144–155.

Kaufman, N., & Lord Larson, V. (2005). *Asperger syndrome: Strategies for solving the social problem.* Eau Claire, WI: Thinking Publications.

Klecan-Aker, J., & Kelty, K. (1990). An investigation of oral narratives of normal and language-learning disabled children. *Journal of Childhood Communication Disorders, 13*, 207–216.

Klinger, L., & Dawson, G. (1992). Facilitating early social and communicative development in children with autism. In S. Warren & J. Reichle (Eds.), *Causes and effects in communication and language intervention* (Vol. 1, pp.157–186). Baltimore: Paul H. Brookes.

Koegel, R., & Koegel, L. (2006). *Pivotal response treatments for autism.* Baltimore: Paul H. Brookes.

Krug, D., Arick, J., & Almond, P. (1993). *Autism Screening Instrument for Educational Planning (Asperger syndrome IEP-2)* (2nd ed.). Austin, TX: Pro-Ed.

Krug, D. A., & Arick, J. R. (2003). *Krug Asperger's Disorder Index (KADI).* Austin, TX: Pro-Ed.

Kuoch, H., & Mirenda, P. (2003). Social story interventions for young children with autism spectrum disorders. *Focus on Autism and Other Developmental Disabilities, 18*, 219–227.

Kuttler, S., Miles, B., & Carson, J. (1999). The use of social stories to reduce precursors to tantrum behavior in a student with autism. *Focus on Autism and Other Developmental Disabilities, 13*, 176–182.

Lahey, M. (1988). *Language disorders and language development.* New York: Macmillian.

Lifter, K., Sulzer-Azaroff, B., Anderson, S., & Cowdery, G. (1993). Teaching play activities to preschool children with disabilities: The importance of developmental considerations. *Journal of Early Intervention, 17,* 139–159.

Lord, C., & Corsello, C. (2005). Diagnostic instruments in autism spectrum disorders. In F. Volkmar, R. Paul, A. Klin, & D. Cohen (Eds.), *Handbook of autism and pervasive developmental disorders: Vol. Two. Assessments, interventions and policy* (pp.730–771). Hoboken, NJ: Wiley.

Lord, C., Rutter, M., DiLavore, P., & Risi, S. (1999). *Autism Diagnostic Observation Scale-WPS* (WPS ed). Los Angeles: Western Psychological Services.

Lovaas, O. I., Schreibman, L., Koegel, R., & Rehm, R. (1971). Selective responding by autistic children to multiple sensory input. *Journal of Abnormal Psychology, 77,* 211–222.

MacIntosh, K., & Dissanayake, C. (2004). Annotation: The similarities and differences between autistic disorder and Asperger's disorder: A review of empirical evidence. *Journal of Child Psychology and Psychiatry, 45,* 421–434.

Manjiviona, J., & Prior, M. (1995). Comparison of Asperger syndrome and high-functioning autistic children on a test of motor impairment. *Journal of Autism and Developmental Disorders, 25,* 23–39.

Marriage, K., Gordon, V., & Brand, L. (1995). A social skills group for boys with Asperger's syndrome. *Australian and New Zealand Journal of Psychiatry, 29,* 58–62.

Mesibov, G., Schopler, E., Schaffer, B., & Landrus, R. (1988). *Adolescent and adult psychoeducational profile (AAPEP).* Austin, TX: Pro-Ed.

Miller, J. N., & Orzonoff, S. (2000). The external validity of Asperger disorder: Lack of evidence from the domain of neuropsychology. *Journal of Abnormal Psychology, 109,* 227–238.

Mirenda, P. (2001). Autism, augmentative communication and assistive technology: What do we really know? *Focus on Autism and Other Developmental Disabilities, 16,* 141–151.

Mirenda, P. (2003). Toward functional augmentative and alternative communication for students with autism: Manual signs, graphic symbols, and voice output communication aides. *Language, Speech, and Hearing Services in Schools, 34,* 202–215.

Morton, K., & Wolford, S. (1994). *Analysis of Sensory Behavior Inventory (ASBI-R)* (rev. ed.). Arcadia, CA: Skills with Occupational Therapy.

Mundy, P. (1995). Joint attention, social-emotional approach in children with autism. *Development and Psychopathology, 7,* 63–82.

Myles, B., & Andreon, C. (2001). *Asperger syndrome: practical solutions for program planning.* Shanwee Mission, KS: Autism Asperger.

Myles, B., Bock, S., & Simpson, R. (2002). *Asperger Syndrome Diagnostic Scale (ASDS)*. Austin, TX: Pro-Ed.

Myles, B., & Simpson, R. (2001). Understanding the hidden curriculum: An essential social skill for children and youth with Asperger syndrome. *Intervention in School and Clinic, 36,* 279–286.

Myles, B., & Simpson, R. (2003). *Asperger syndrome: A guide for educators and parents* (2nd ed.). Austin, TX: Pro-Ed.

National Research Council. (2001). *Educating children with autism.* Washington, DC: National Academy Press, Committee on Educational Interventions for Children with Autism, Division of Behavioral and Social Sciences and Education.

Neisworth, J., & Wolfe, P. (2005). *The autism encyclopedia.* Baltimore: Paul H. Brookes.

Orzonoff, S., & Miller, J. (1995). Teaching theory of mind: A new approach to social skills training for individuals with autism. *Journal of Autism and Developmental Disorders, 25,* 415–433.

Pangborn, J., & Baker, S. (2001). *Biomedical assessment options for children autism and related problems: A consensus report of Defeat Autism Now!* San Diego, CA: Autism Research Institute.

Partington, J. W., & Sundberg, M. (1998). *Assessment of Basic Language and Learning Skills (ABLLS)*. Pleasant Hill, CA: Behavior Analysts Incorporated.

Prizant, B. (1983). Language acquisition and communicative behavior in autism: Toward an understanding of the "whole" of it. *Journal of Speech and Language Disorders, 48,* 296–307.

Randall, P., & Parker, J. (1999). *Supporting the families of children with autism.* Chichester, Toronto: John Wiley & Sons.

Rellini, E., Tortolani, D., Trillo, S., Carbone, S., & Montecchi, F. (2004). Childhood Autism Rating Scale (CARS) and Autism Behavior Checklist (ABC): Correspondence and conflicts with the DSM-IV (2000) criteria in the diagnosis of autism. *Journal of Autism and Developmental Disorders, 34,* 703–708.

Reynolds, C., & Kamphaus, R. (1992). *Behavior Assessment System for Children (BASC)*. Circle Pines, MN: American Guidance Services.

Richard, G., & Hanner, M. (2005). *The Language Processing Test—3* (3rd ed.). East Moline, IL: LinguiSystems.

Riley, A. M. (1994). *Evaluating Acquired Skills in Communication (EASIC-R)* (rev. ed.). Austin, TX: Pro-Ed.

Robins, D., Fein, D., Barton, M., & Green, J. (2001). The Modified Checklist for Autism in Toddlers: An initial study investigating the early detection of autism and pervasive developmental disorders. *Journal of Autism and Developmental Disorders, 31,* 131–151.

Roid, G., & Miller, L. (2002). *Leiter International Performance Scale* (rev. ed.). Wood Dale, IL: Stoelting Co.

Rutter, M., Bailey, A., & Lord, C. (2003). *Social Communication Questionnaire (SCQ)*. Los Angeles: Western Psychological Services.

Rutter, M., LeCouteur, A., & Lord, C. (2003). *Autism Diagnostic Interview (ADI-R)* (rev. ed.). Los Angeles: Western Psychological Services.

Rutter, M., LeCouteur, A., & Lord, C. (2003). *Manual for the Autism Diagnostic Interview* (WPS version). Los Angeles: Western Psychological Services.

Sachs, O. (1995). *An anthropologist on Mars: Seven paradoxical tales.* New York: Alfred A. Knopf.

Schafer Autism Report. (2006). *Number of children in CA doubles.* Retrieved September 14, 2006, from http://www.sarnet.org.

Schlosser, R. (2003, November). *Evidenced-based practice in augmentative and alternative communication.* Invited presentation at the American Speech-Language-Hearing Association Convention, Chicago.

Schlosser, R., & Lee, D. (2000). Promoting generalization and maintenance in augmentative and alternative communication: A meta-analysis of 20 years effectiveness research. *Augmentative and Alternative Communication, 16,* 208–227.

Schopler, E., Reichler, R., Bashford, A., Lansing, M., & Marcus, L. (in press). *Psychoeducational Profile (PEP-3)* (3rd rev.). Austin, TX: Pro-Ed.

Schopler, E., Reichler, R., & Renner, B. (1988). *The Childhood Autism Rating Scale (CARS).* Los Angeles: Western Psychological Services.

Schopler, E., Reichler, R., & Renner, B. (1988). *Childhood Autism Rating Scale (CARS).* Los Angeles, CA: Western Psychological Services.

Seigel, B. (2004). *Pervasive Developmental Disorders Screening Test* (2nd ed.). San Antonio, TX: Psychological Corporation.

Siegel, D., Minshew, N.,& Goldstein, G. (1996). Weschler IQ profiles in the diagnosis of high-functioning autism. *Journal of Autism and Developmental Disorders, 26,* 389-406.

Simpson, R. (2001). ABA and students with autism spectrum disorders: Issues and considerations for effective practice. *Focus on Autism and Other Developmental Disorders, 16,* 68–71.

Simpson, R. (2005). Evidence-based practices and students with autism spectrum disorders. *Focus on Autism and Other Developmental Disabilities, 20*(3), 140–149.

Smith, I., & Bryson, D. (1994). Imitation and action in autism: a critical review. *Psychological Bulletin, 116,* 259-273.

South, M., Williams, B., MacMahon, W., Owely, T., Filipek, P., Shernoff, E., et al. (2002). Utility of the Gilliam Autism Rating Scale in research and clinical populations. *Journal of Autism and Developmental Disorders, 32,* 593–599.

Sparrow, S. S., Balla, D. A., & Cicchetti, D. V. (1998). *Vineland Social-Emotional Childhood Scales (SEEC)*. Circle Pines, MN: American Guidance Service.

Squires, J., Bricker, D., & Twombly, E. (with Yockelson, S., Davis, M. S., & Kim, Y.). (2002). *Ages and Stages Questionnaires: Social-Emotional: A parent-completed, child-monitoring system for social-emotional behaviors (ASQ:SE)*. Baltimore: Paul H. Brookes.

Squires, J., Potter, L., & Bricker, D. (1999). *The ASQ user's guide for the Ages and Stages Questionnaires: A parent-completed, child monitoring system* (2nd. ed.). Baltimore: Paul H. Brookes.

Stanford, P., & Siders, J. (2001). Authentic assessment for intervention. *Intervention in School and Clinic, 36*, 163–167.

Stewart, C. (2004). *Family stories of Asperger syndrome*. Unpublished manuscript, Radford University, Radford, VA.

Stone, W., Coonrod, E., & Ousley, O. (2000). Brief report: Screening Tool for Autism in Two-Year-Olds (STAT): Development and preliminary data. *Journal of Autism and Developmental Disorders, 30*, 607–612.

Stone, W., Coonrod, E., Turner, L., & Pozdol, S. (2004). Psychometric properties of the STAT for early autism screening. *Journal of Autism and Developmental Disorders, 34*, 691–701.

Stone, W., & Ousley, O. (1997). *STAT manual: Screening Tool for Autism in Two-Year Olds*. Unpublished manuscript, Vanderbilt University, Nashville, TN.

Sundbye, N. (2001). *Assessing the struggling reader: What to look for and how to make sense of it*. Lawrence, KS: Curriculum Solutions.

Swicegood, P. (1994). Portfolio-based assessment practices: The uses of portfolio assessment for students with behavioral disorders or learning disabilities. *Intervention School and Clinic, 30*, 6–15.

Tsai, L. (2000). Children with autism spectrum disorders: Medicine today and in the new millennium. *Focus on Autism and Other Developmental Disabilities, 15*, 138–145.

Volkmar, F., & Klin, A. (2000). Diagnostic issues. In A. Klin, F. Volkmar, & S. Sparrow (Eds.), *Asperger syndrome* (pp. 25–71). New York: Guilford Press.

Volkmar, F., Lord, C., Bailey, A., Schultz, R., & Klin, A. (2004). Autism and pervasive developmental disorders. *Journal of Child Psychology and Psychiatry, 45*, 135–170.

Watters, A. (2005). *Theory of mind and children with Asperger syndrome*. Unpublished master's thesis, Radford University, Radford, VA.

Wendt, O., Schlosser, R. & Lloyd, L. (2002, November). *AAC for children with autism: A meta analysis for intervention*. Paper presented at the American Speech-Language-Hearing Association Annual Convention, Atlanta, GA.

Wetherby, A., & Prizant, B. (2002). *Communication and Symbolic Behavior Scales—Developmental Profile.* (1st normed ed.). Baltimore: Paul H. Brookes.

Wetherby, A., Woods, J., Allen, L., Cleary, J., Dickinson, H., & Lord, C. (2004). Early indicators of autism spectrum disorders in the second year of life. *Journal of Autism and Developmental Disorders, 34,* 473–493.

Wiig, E., & Secord, W. (1989). *The Test of Language Competence* (expanded ed.). San Antonio, TX: Psychological Corp.

Williams, D. (1992). *Nobody nowhere: The extraordinary autobiography of an autistic.* New York: Avon Books.

Williams, D. (1994). *Somebody somewhere: Breaking free from the world of autism.* New York: Times Books.

Wing, L. (1981). Asperger's syndrome: A clinical account. *Psychological Medicine, 11,* 115–119.

Wing, L. (1996). *The autistic spectrum: A guide for parents and professionals.* London: Constable.

Wing, L. (1998). The history of Asperger syndrome. In E. Schopler, G. Mesibov, & L. Kunce (Eds.), *Asperger's syndrome or high functioning autism?* (pp. 11–28). New York: Plenum Press.

Zachman, L., Barrett, M., Huisingh, R., Orman, J., & Blagden, C. (1991). *Test of Problem Solving—Adolescent.* East Moline, IL: LinguiSystems.

Zachman, L., Huisingh, R., Barrett, M., Orman, J., & LoGiudice, C. (1994). *Test of Problem Solving—Elementary* (rev. ed.). East Moline, IL: LinguiSystems.

Zeitlin, S., Williamson, G. G., & Szczepanski, M. (1988). *Early Coping Inventory (ECI).* Bensenville, IL: Scholastic Testing Service.

Index

A

AAC (Augmentative and Alternative Communication), 73–74
AAPEP (Adolescent and Adult Psychoeducational Profile), 55, 56
ABLLS (Assessment of Basic Language and Learning Skills), 57
Academic skills
  Asperger syndrome and, 38–46
    reading, 40–41
  autism and, 25–26
ADI-R (Autism Diagnostic Interview, Revised), 53, 57
Adolescent/Adult Sensory Profile, 56
Adolescent and Adult Psychoeducational Profile (AAPEP), 55, 56
Adolescent Treatment Program at the Meninger Clinic, 10
ADOS (Autism Diagnostic Observation Schedule), 53, 57
Ages & Stages Questionnaires, 56
Analysis of Sensory Behavior Inventory, Revised Edition, 56
ASDS (Asperger Syndrome Diagnostic Scale), 54, 56
Asperger syndrome, 9–12
  academic skills and, 38–46
    narrative skills, 41–46
    reading, 40–41

    writing, 41
  assessment of, informal, 66–67
  characteristics of, 9–12
  cognitive abilities and, 31–33
  description/diagnosis of, 12–14, 30, 67–68
  diagnostic tools, 53–66
  language abilities and, 33–35
  related problems, 10
  sensory/motor skills and, 36–38
  social abilities and, 35–36
  treatments for, 70–72
Asperger Syndrome Diagnostic Scale (ASDS), 54, 56
ASQ (Autism Screening Questionnaire), 58
Assessment, autism, 50–51
Assessment of Basic Language and Learning Skills (ABLLS), 57
Augmentative and Alternative Communication (AAC), 73–74
Autism
  academic skills and, 25–26
  assessment of, informal, 66–67
  behavioral symptoms of, 6, 8–9
  cognitive abilities and, 16–19
  defined, 2–3
  description of, 7–8
  developmental domains affected by, 3
  diagnosis of, 50–51, 67–68
  diagnostic tools, 53–66